we hope this fills many hours
of interesting reading   many happy
returns

James & Barbara
Jamie & Sarah Jane.
5-18-91.

THE SHOOTING FIELD
with
HOLLAND & HOLLAND

Harris Holland, a portrait in the possession of the Holland family.

THE SHOOTING FIELD

with

HOLLAND & HOLLAND

Revised and enlarged edition

Peter King

Quiller Press

DEDICATION

This book is dedicated to GUNMAKERS

'The gunmaker is something of a multiple
personality at the best of times, for, in point of fact,
an arm is seldom made by any one man. The
gunmaker himself knows how to execute most of
the work of the various departments. He was, in a
word, the master craftsman who supervised the
whole and often put the finishing touches. An arm
should be looked on as the work of his particular
school or shop – full of skilled craftsmen.'

Hugh P. C. Pollard

First published MCMLXXXV by Quiller Press Ltd
46 Lillie Road, London SW6 1TN

Revised and Enlarged Edition 1990

Published in the United States by
Blacksmith Corporation, Southport, Connecticut, USA

Copyright © MCMLXXXV Holland & Holland
ISBN 1 870948 39 4
U.S. Library of Congress Number 85-19109

List of Contents

This picture of a .410 double shotgun was printed in the Sunday
Telegraph *having been chosen by Mr D. J. Penn as the 'Weapon'
representative for the journal's selection of the most beautiful products
of British industry.*

THE MOST BEAUTIFUL *WEAPON*
Chosen by
D. J. PENN
Keeper of Weapons in the Imperial War Museum

A weapon's beauty must spring from more than just embellishment. If it is not functional, it ceases to be a weapon, becoming something else, an article of male jewellery perhaps. Excessive adornment may even impair efficiency. I have therefore eschewed Italian parade armour, French smallswords and Scottish pistols, splendid decorative pieces though they are. Longbows, duelling pistols and Japanese swords possesses lethal elegance, but their time has passed. By contrast, the English 'best' shotgun remains in hard and widespread use.

No more magnificent example of the 100-year-old design could be found than this Holland & Holland gun. There is not a redundant line on the weapon. It carries no excess weight and every part functions smoothly and unobtrusively.

Made to measure for its owners, it operates in perfect harmony with him. It is as deadly as a panther. The engraving is breathtaking in concept and execution, yet interferes not a whit with the gun's performance.

The weapon stands alone as the epitome of the English sporting gun today, a harmonious combination not only of functional and decorative beauty but traditional craft skills and the consummate ability of the Brown brothers, the engravers, who are only in their mid-twenties.

Author's Preface

What does *The Shooting Field* mean? To one man it means the grouse moors on 12th August. To another a field of English crops on 1st September. To a third, it may mean memories of shooting tigers from the backs of elephants, or the other way about, whichever you find most pleasing as Lord Curzon told The Souls. To yet another man it may call up recollections of Bisley. To the legendary Colonel Hawker it would, 'in its most enjoyable form, mean a north-easter with the thermometer below zero, a punt gun, and only half an inch of plank between himself and eternity'. We take these remarks from Teasdale-Buckell's classic written in 1900. He goes on to describe other shooting men for whom the phrase calls up 'recollections of hard gallops after American bison and the deadly work of the revolver, or its kindred African sport of riding down the giraffe'. Well, those are things of the past, but not alas, is the form of shooting 'in which the object is to pierce the strongest steel armour plates' in the field of battle.

So to write about *The Shooting Field* presents this difficulty, that the words mean different things to different readers. A difficulty should always provide an opportunity and we have taken this to be the chance to cover a wide canvas. We make no apology for quoting from the greatest shots because they alone are able to write with the brilliance that comes from natural genius. Take Colonel Hawker. 'Joe shot like an angel; he discharged ten rounds and pocketed his ten birds in brilliant style. What care we for all Europe?'

Our aim is not to compete with this but merely to describe some of the interests of shooting through the experiences of Holland & Holland, and to quote shooting men of distinction who have written vividly on the subject, particularly those who used Holland guns over the years from 1835. In the hope that the book will be of general interest to Holland's customers and friends, it therefore deals as much with the background to shooting over this period as it does with the minutiae of the firm's guns and business.

First and foremost we acknowledge a debt of gratitude to those members of Holland & Holland who have provided help with the text, both as regards the guns and the business, and also the Holland family who have been generous with memories and archives. Mr. Horace West was kind enough to provide essential background to the company's activities; and

Members of the Holland family.

Mr. Steve Vogel has been generous in his support of the book throughout. We are also grateful to the many authors, long dead, from whom we quote, and to those listed whose publishers have given permission for quotation. Mr. William Husselby has given generously of his facilities and his advice; Mrs. Cherry Carroll has helped with paper restoration and given her support; Miss Eunice Wilson deciphered some of the Hollands' handwriting, and Ms Sandra den Hertog deciphered some of the author's handwriting before typing the manuscript.

The book was originally conceived as part of the celebrations connected with the 150th anniversary in 1985 of the founding of the company. When the time came for reprinting, the opportunity was taken to update the history section. We are grateful for the comments received from Mr. Jeffrey Holland who has made an extensive study of the genealogy of the Holland family and some of his observations have been incorporated in the text. The author also acknowledges with thanks the assistance provided by Geoffrey Boothroyd in providing the text on W. J. Jeffrey & Co.

Peter King

'You made a hundred runs in best cricket'

Holland & Holland 1835–1905

Henry Holland.

'You as a firm stand for the very best and finest points in the British gun trade.' That is certainly something when it is spoken by a Purdey. And it was Tom Purdey, speechmaking at Holland & Holland's centenary celebrations fifty years ago, who went on to quote from his father's telegram of congratulations to Hollands, read out at the same beano at the Connaught Rooms in London, which said, 'You have made a hundred runs in best cricket.' Purdey junior explained that this, translated, meant 'that you have had 100 years of the very highest and unblemished reputation as a firm. I have never heard anything detrimental of your firm.'

Tom Purdey also referred to the late Henry Holland, who, after the founder, had been the great architect of the success of the business in that first 100 years. He had, said Purdey, done more for the whole gun trade than anyone else, and had worked hand-in-hand with Purdey's own father 'to bring about the efficiency and fairness of the proof houses in London and probably in Birmingham too. They worked together and they produced all sorts of very difficult things at very difficult times' . . . and so on.

To understand the background to all this, we must leave the Connaught Rooms and go back in time to 1835, but not far away in London, to nearby King Street, Holborn, to where Harris Holland set up his business at No. 9. That year, 1835, was a dramatic time, being the very year in which the most famous of all gunmakers, Joseph Manton, had died in poverty. This is not the place to eulogise Manton, except to note that since almost all gunmakers had worked for him at one time or another, or worked for those who had already worked for him, the best word to describe the trade in the 1830s was incestuous. Even Manton's brother had been foreman for the famous Twigg. Manton was in prison for debt in 1829 and he died in 1835 at the age of 69. 'From wealth, therefore, he was reduced to want, by the assistance of lawyers and the patent laws,' Colonel Hawker wrote. He also wrote an inscription on his stone:

'To the memory of Joseph Manton, who died, universally regretted, on the 29th day of June 1835, aged sixty-nine. This humble tablet is placed here by his afflicted family, merely to mark where are deposited his mortal remains. But one everlasting monument to his unrivalled genius is already established in every quarter of the globe, by his celebrity as the greatest artist in firearms that ever the world produced; as the founder and father of the modern gun trade, and as a most scientific inventor in other departments, not only for the benefit of his friends and the sporting world, but for the good of his king and country.'

Manton's tomb now sadly delapidated, erected in 1835, the year Harris Holland founded the business.

Purdey had worked for Manton after 1805 but three years later went into business with the famous Dr Forsyth. In 1814 he set up on his own in Princes Street, off Leicester Square, and then in 1826 in Manton's former premises at 314½ Oxford Street (where D. H. Evans store now stands). Lancaster, who had been barrel-boring for Manton, set up business also in 1826. Thomas Boss, another Manton man, who also worked for Purdey, commenced business for himself in 1830 at 3 Grosvenor Street, then moved to Clifford Street and then to St James's. When Boss died, Mrs Boss took into the firm Stephen Grant, who also later set up on his own, a few doors away in St James's. Later, Boss's nephew took on James Robertson, whose father had first fitted telescopes to rifles, and who had worked for Sir Joseph Whitworth in Manchester and Westley Richards in Birmingham. Later he worked for Purdeys and co-operated with Holland.

Harris Holland therefore had the somewhat dubious distinction of never working for Manton, or for a Manton disciple, and appears to have been his own man throughout. There are unsubstantiated stories in the gun trade that some of Holland's earliest guns were made for him by Boss, and later by Robertson who, as indicated above, had worked for the Boss firm after Thomas died. A more likely account of his beginnings is given in a letter from a relative of the Hollands (she was a first cousin of the Hollands because her grandmother – Miss Cowper – was also their grandmother) who says, 'As a young girl I was to all intents and purposes adopted by Uncle Harris and Aunt Eliza. I was more than half my time with them. He, Uncle Harris, was very musical and intended for a musical career. He was however a magnificent shot – sport and art rarely amalgamate! Music seems to have been a wash-out and someone, I've a vague idea it was the King of Italy, backed him financially and so the Bond Street shop came into existance and flourished.' Commenting on this, Albert Madell, who joined Holland & Holland as an office boy in May 1919 and thus worked under Henry Holland for more than a decade, says, 'Harris Holland's hobby was making firearms. He was so talented that the customers of his tobacco shop urged him to adopt gun-making as a living which he did with their financial help. (Certainly) someone who recognised his genius (for he was that without doubt) induced him to change his vocation to that of gunmaker. I am pretty sure that it was not the King of Italy, though I remember that His Majesty was a good customer of the firm, as was the Queen.'

Harris John Holland was the son of an organ builder, who married a Miss Cowper, who is variously described as having come from Hertfordshire or Bedfordshire, and who died about 1870. Harris Holland, born in 1806, married Elizabeth Marshall in 1840. They had two girls, Lizzie and Annie, but no sons.

Holland & Holland's factory overlooks the Kensal Green Cemetery where Manton is buried.

Later, it appears that Harris Holland married, probably in the 1850s, a second time Charlotte Frederica. She died on 2nd March, 1896 at Greville Place, Kilburn, aged 90.

Holland was a tobacconist – a wholesale tobacconist it is believed – and in 1835 he was trading from 9 King Street, a busy commercial street in Holborn, now incorporated into and renamed Southampton Row. Early on he became a well-known sportsman and a fine shot, one of the frequenters of the Old Red House and Hornsey Wood, which were fashionable London pigeon-shooting clubs, and where he would have met James Purdey, also a keen shot. Later, when he was more affluent, he rented the Edmund Byers moors in Durham, for a period of 30 years at a rent of £100 per annum. In turn, he rented them out as subscription moors.

Harris Holland frequented Hornsey Wood pigeon-shooting club, a fashionable venue.

LEFT: *98 Bond Street, where Henry Holland moved in 1866. It was part club, part gun room, part shop.*

John Holland – as he then called himself – probably traded in guns as well as making them in these early days, because it is not until the 1848 Commercial Directory that he describes himself as a gunmaker as well as a tobacconist. By 1857, when he was 52, he has taken to using the full name Harris John Holland and to describing himself as a gunmaker, dropping the tobacconist. To add to the confusion, Harris John had two brothers, one called John and the other William Henry. At that time there were over 90 other gunmakers listed in London, as well as specialist firms of gun-barrel makers, gun-case makers, gun-engravers, gun-flint makers, gun-implement makers, gun-lock makers and polishers, gun-stock makers, gun-wadding manufacturers and gun-barrel browners.

Why did Harris Holland go into this highly competitive business of London gunmaking at this time? What kind of guns did he make? The answers must be, as Madell said, that he was without doubt a genius of a kind, using the skills he would have inherited from his father, the organ builder, to design and make guns which his friends and customers recognised as being his true vocation in life. Because he had no sons of his own, it was understandable that he would take his nephew, Henry, under his wing. Known as Henry William, the nephew is believed to be the son of William Henry, although Mr. Jeffrey Holland has suggested that Henry William's father may have been John, Harris John's other brother. William Henry was a solicitor and he and Harris John married sisters. Harris first invited Henry to shoot on the Durham grouse moors when he was 14, and each year afterwards Henry shot there until he gave up shooting. Henry Holland (born in 1845,) was 15 when he was apprenticed to his uncle. As his Indentures show, Henry was paid a wage of four shillings a week in the first year, increasing to 15 shillings a week over the last two years of his seven-year apprenticeship. Throughout this period he would have lived over the shop. In 1866 or thereabouts Harris Holland moved from Holborn to more prestigious premises at 98 New Bond Street, near Brook Street, where he had a dressmaker called Madame Bonaparte as neighbour on one side, and another dressmaker and a tailor on the other. As we have already heard it was suggested that one of his customers – perhaps the King of Italy – put up the money for the Bond Street lease. *

In 1867, on the completion of his apprenticeship, Henry Holland appears to have become an effective partner in the firm, although no formal agreements of a legal nature dated before 1876 now exist. Sometime in that decade, the name of the firm was changed to Holland & Holland. Perhaps Harris Holland formally retired from day to day control in 1876 at the age of 70, and it was because of this that he had the formal partnership agreement drawn up. That June, Harris signed the lengthy agreement with Henry, by which the latter would pay £1500 by instalments for the benefit of the partnership. A new arrangement began from 1st January 1880 under which the Bond Street premises, then on a 21-year lease, should be 'the sole property' of Harris Holland; in exchange for giving up his share in the shop, Henry was absolved from all further payments of the balance of the £1000 still outstanding from the 1876 agreement. Furthermore, during the first seven years of the new partnership Harris was to have 'two equal third parts' of the net profits and Henry 'the remaining equal third'. After seven years Harris was to have four equal seventh parts and Henry the balance of three sevenths. Harris could take £100 out of the business each calendar month and Henry £50.

By January 1884, it had been agreed between the partners that they share the net profits equally. Although it has been said that Harris Holland retired in 1876, he appears to have remained an active partner in the sense that Henry Holland kept in close contact with him, and we have copies of their business correspondence – or part of it – up to 1896 when Harris died.

The relationship between them appears to have been a formal one but there is little doubt that the uncle recognised the capabilities of his junior partner. Madell once said: 'Henry Holland made the firm even more famous because he was a first-class shot with a rifle and won lots of competitions at Bisley.' However Harris clearly never relinquished control of the business, even though he had theoretically retired. For example in 1896 Harris received the following letter from his nephew:

My dear Uncle,
I enclose a letter re cheques. I am sorry that you are ill but trust you will soon be better enough to transact business.
     I would point out that my not having the power to sign cheques has been a kind of reflection upon me, considering

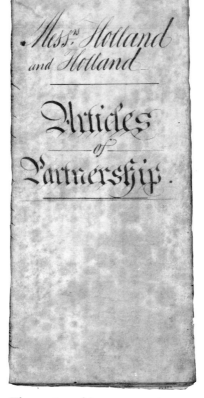

The partnership agreement between Harris Holland and his nephew Henry.

---

*At one time, there were no less than twelve gunmakers in the street, and opposite No 98 was a butchers with a chopping block outside.

that I have been nearly forty years [in it] and been a partner for about twenty years . . . If I were a signatory to the firm's cheques but they are to be initialled by someone else, the position would be still more uncomplimentary to me. It is extremely awkward that you are not able to come up here and arrange important matters of business. I don't even know that the letters are read by you. I think that as soon as you are a little better I had better come and see you and settle things on a permanent basis.
Yours affectionately.

The year before he died, the business had grown to such an extent that Holland & Holland bought or leased the Baptist Chapel numbered 527 to 533 Harrow Road, near the Halfpenny Steps (so-called because it was close to the footbridge over the Grand Union Canal which ran behind the building, and for which a toll charge of one halfpenny was made). This building, which still stands, was only a few hundred yards from the present factory, close to the junction of the Harrow Road and Ladbroke Grove*.

Certainly Henry Holland was proud of the factory, which he described as 'equipped with the most modern appliances, at a cost of about £10,000, with a floor area of over 15,000 sq ft or double the capacity of the old works, with ground available for further extension should the same be required.' It was built on a piece of land he bought for £850 on a lease from All Souls College, Oxford, with 87 years unexpired at a ground rent of only £2 a year.

His first action, when he eventually assumed control on his uncle's death, was to make Mr Froome his partner, in appreciation of the valuable services he had given since taking up an apprenticeship 40 years previously around 1855. A contemporary account explains that it was 'in 1883 when the late Mr Walsh held a rifle trial in London that Mr Froome became celebrated in the eyes of sportsmen, and especially those who were fortunate enough to stalk the red stag in Scotland, or invade the Indian or African solitudes in search of big game'.

The partnership with Froome was rather one-sided. In an agreement made on 11th November 1896 Henry Holland noted that he had 'some time since agreed to admit [Mr Froome] who has for many years been employed as a Manager . . . as a salaried partner with him in such business with a contingent percentage upon certain contemplated increased profits.' Henry retained his ownership of the goodwill of the business and of all the capital assets and property including the freehold premises in the Harrow Road (the 'old' factory) and the leasehold premises at 98 New Bond Street and the leases of the Shooting Grounds. Henry was also 'entitled to the whole of the profits of the business' and was to have 'the custody and sole rights of access to the private ledger containing the balance sheets of the business and such ledgers shall be his private property, and he shall have the sole power to sign cheques etc.'

---

*It is something of a mystery why, only three years later, Henry Holland should have moved up the road to the purpose-built factory in which the firm makes its guns to this day.

Mr Froome's benefits were confined to the following:
(1) a salary of £750 p.a.
(2) 7½ per cent of the sum by which the annual profits exceeded one half of the net profits in the years 1894 and 1895.

Finally 'in all matters connected with the general direction and superintendance of the business, the opinions and directions of the said Henry William Holland shall prevail [and Mr Froome] shall have no authority with respect thereto in opposition to the directions of Mr Holland.'

When Henry moved into the new, purpose-built factory, he imported from Birmingham a considerable number of skilled gunmakers, and housed them in properties he bought for the purpose in the surrounding streets. New housing was being built at the time on the other side of the main London Midland & Scottish Railway line that ran along one side of the factory. These Birmingham men in turn brought their sons, the next generation of craftsmen, to work in the factory after the first world war, and they too lived in company houses until the 1960s. Having secured new factory premises, a cadre of skilled workmen, and assured the continued loyalty of Mr. Froome, Henry Holland now turned his attention to his most pressing problem – how to provide working capital, since his uncle had left him with none. In a letter of April 2nd 1898, he set out the problem, and its possible solution, in a letter to a business adviser, probably Sir Ralph Payne-Gallwey.

Mr Froome, one of the great shots of the century, became Henry Holland's partner.

Apr 2 '98   Private and confidential

Dear Sir

I rather wanted to have half an hour's conversation with you but perhaps can write and explain.

You have always been so good a friend to me personally as well as to my firm that I take the liberty of asking I won't say your advice – rather your opinion on the following –

The capital in this business is a large one and the larger proportion of this capital belonged to my late uncle and partner who died in March '96. Upon his death the whole of the business became mine – but I had to pay out the capital of the deceased to his exectrs. The result is that all my eggs are in one basket – a very good basket certainly – but it makes it exceedingly difficult to make a will when one has a wife and children as well as others depending upon one. Now I am advised by my solicitors and friends to turn the concern into a private – or semi private – company – retaining the ordinary share myself so that I should still have more interest than anyone else in the prosperity of the business – but issuing 5% well secured Preference shares to my customers. When I say well secured I mean that the properties belonging to the business should exceed the amount of the Preference shares issued made up of Patents, goodwill etc – & that the profits of the business as shown for the last three years should cover the Preference interest about four times over – The business turnover increases rapidly & so do the profits in proportion.

The properties would consist of items – valued at £68106 roughly – as per enclosed.

I could sell the whole for a very large sum – but I have no wish to do this as I only want to dispose of the Preference shares & to keep the ordinary – so that I should still be more interested in the success of the business than anyone else.

Under the circumstances I cannot think that turning my business into a company can have any detrimental effect – on the contrary it should improve business as so many of my customers would take shares & feel a direct interest in the success – as has been the case with many good substantial businesses turned into companies during the last few years. Always on the understanding that the late proprietor keeps sufficient capital in to make it his interest to do his best.

My new factory is just finished – when all is cleaned up the total cost will have been to me £10,000. It is far and away the best of its kind in England & should facilitate the manufacture of guns in every way – Kindly return enclosed when you have read it & I should be obliged if for the present you would consider this & the enclosure, strongly confidential.

Trusting that you will not think that I am encroaching upon your good nature in writing to you upon this subject. I am your obedient servant

PS Please reply to 28 Maida Vale London W

This letter must have been one of the few occasions when Holland unburdened himself, because a friend says of him at this time:

'In conversation with him it is easy to discover a man of the world; one who watches for the turn of the tide of fashion and is ever ready to meet it . . . Not that it is easy (he goes on) to discover his secret thoughts, for we are not quite sure that Mr Holland does not, to some extent, subscribe to Tallyrand's view that language was given to him in order to conceal his thoughts. Business is business, and it would never do to enlighten everybody upon what is going to take place the day after tomorrow; nor how a good gunmaker prepares to meet it.'

By July, however, Holland was ready to announce his plans and *The Times* wrote as follows on 2nd July: 'We understand that the old-established firm of Holland & Holland, the well-known gunmakers of New Bond Street, is about to be registered as a limited company, and a prospectus will be issued shortly.'

The Field was somewhat more effusive:

'We understand that this highly successful business of Holland and Holland, the well-known gun manufacturers of New Bond Street is, for family reasons, about to be converted into a limited company. The business will be conducted in the same manner as heretofore, Mr Henry Holland, as chairman, and Mr William Froome, as a director, continuing the management of the firm, assisted by the same managers of departments and staff that have brought the business to the prominent position it now holds in the sporting world. We believe that practically the whole of the ordinary shares will be taken by the firm, they thereby showing their confidence in the continued success of the business. A certain number of preference shares will be issued, and we are informed that customers of the firm will receive special consideration and attention.'

And *Land and Water* (now defunct but famous in its day) added: 'The new company will deserve the support of sportsmen.'

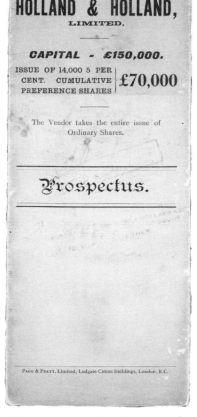

The prospectus for the issue of shares 1898.

The 'new' factory at 906 Harrow Road at the turn of the century.

The position was that Henry Holland, while retaining control of the business, was capitalising it to a total of £150,000 made up of 30,000 shares of £5 each, of which 16,000 would be ordinary shares held by the vendors, and the remainder Preference shares, the proceeds of the sale of many of the latter also going to Mr Holland. The firm was in a strong position. Its reputation, certainly since *The Field* trials 15 years before (see p. 36), was virtually unrivalled, and average annual profits for the past three years had been over £12,000.

On 5th July a quorum of directors met and approved the memorandum and articles of association. The prospectus for the issue of 14,000 5 per cent cumulative preference shares of £5 each was also approved. The take-up was speedy and enthusiastic, and on 8th July a further meeting of directors approved the share allotment. The 79 shareholders comprised several described as 'gentlemen', 'esquires' and 'landowners' as well as a good many military men and successful businessmen – a cross section of the firm's customers, which Henry Holland estimated then totalled 12,000.

The Financier reported that

'taking the previous year's profits as a basis, the Preference dividend was covered nearly four times over. It was certified that for the past seven years, the average profits per annum

The factory today.

had been £11,098, for the last three years it had averaged to £12,041 and in the past year it had been £13,128. Assets were valued at £72,533 exclusive of goodwill, patents, trademarks, etc.'

This successful launch of the business was unquestionably a personal triumph for Henry Holland, and was to secure its welfare for the next sixty years, despite a virtual social revolution (after 1918) and an economic depression which would cause many other gunmakers to go under. Once the arrangements for the new company had been finalised, it was time to regularise Henry Holland's own position, and on 1st January 1903 the board formally appointed him managing director at a salary of £1000 per annum plus 25 per cent of the net profits, after 8 per cent had been paid as dividend on the Ordinary shares, and all Preference share dividends paid.

Three years later, at the end of 1905, at a Directors' meeting 'upon the proposal of Mr W. G. Rayner seconded by Mr Thos. Woodward, Mr Harry Robert Holland was elected a director of the company at a remuneration of £100 per annum'. This was Hal, Henry Holland's eldest son, who it was assumed would take over from his father (now 60 years old) when the time for his retirement came. But, as we shall see, things did not work out like that.

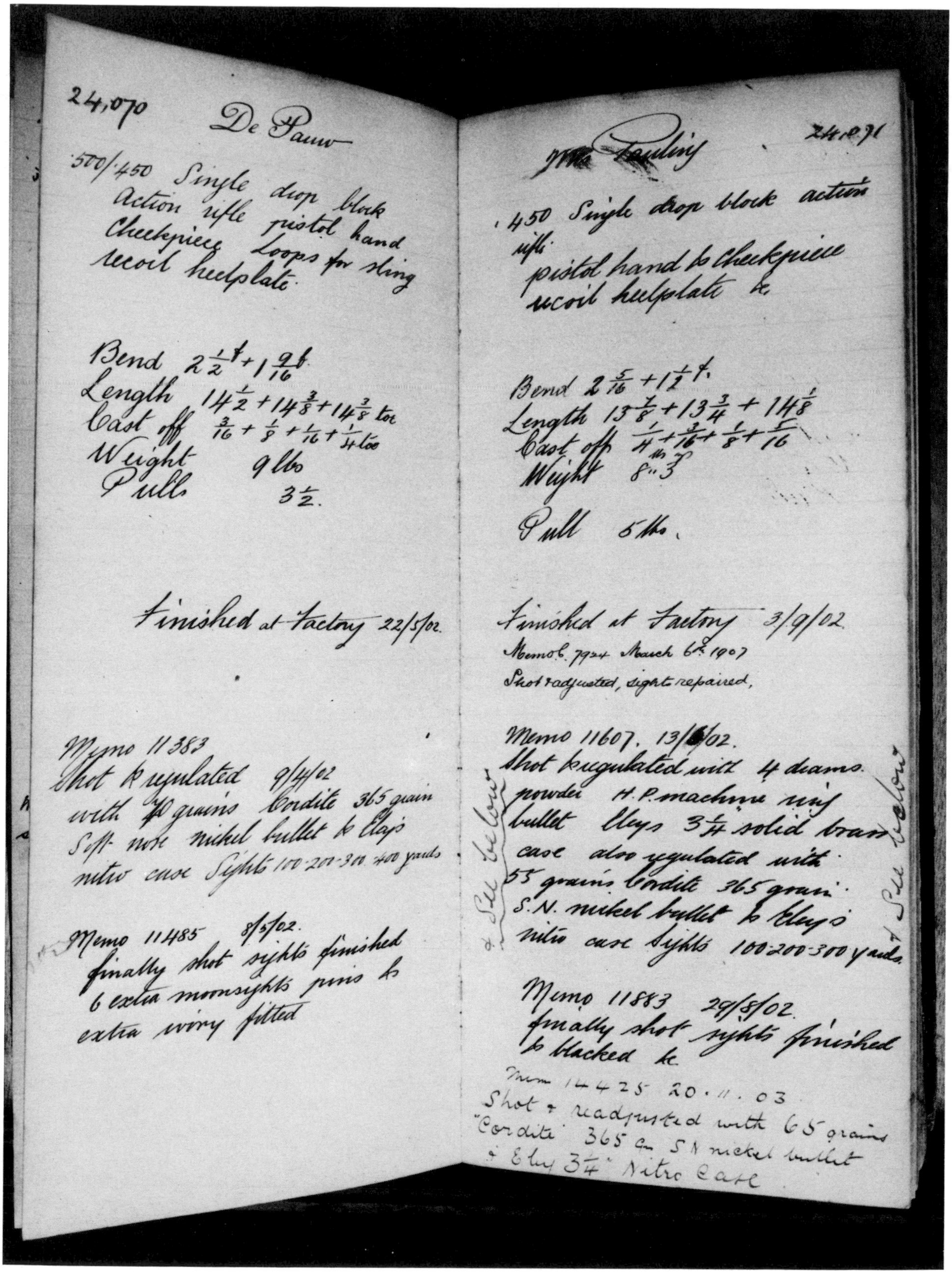

24,070   De Pauw

·500/450 Single drop block
Action rifle pistol hand
Cheekpiece Loops for sling
recoil heelplate

Bend $2\frac{1}{2} + 1\frac{9}{16}$

Length $14\frac{1}{2} + 14\frac{3}{8} + 14\frac{3}{8}$ toe

Cast off $\frac{3}{16} + \frac{1}{8} + \frac{1}{16} + \frac{1}{4}$ too

Weight   9 lbs

Pull $3\frac{1}{2}$.

Finished at Factory 22/5/02.

Memo 11383
Shot & regulated   9/4/02
with 70 grains Cordite 365 grain
Soft nose nickel bullet & Eley's
nitro case Sights 100·200·300 400 yards

Memo 11485   8/5/02.
finally shot sights finished
6 extra moonsights pins &
extra ivory fitted

Wm Pauling   24,071

·450 Single drop block action
rifle
pistol hand & cheekpiece
recoil heelplate &c

Bend $2\frac{5}{16} + 1\frac{1}{2}$ t.

Length $15\frac{7}{8} + 13\frac{3}{4} + 14\frac{1}{8}$

Cast off $\frac{1}{4} + \frac{3}{16} + \frac{1}{8} + \frac{1}{16}$

Weight   8"3

Pull   5 lbs.

Finished at Factory 3/9/02.
Memo C 7924 March 6th 1907
Shot & adjusted, sight repaired,

Memo 11607. 13/8/02.
Shot & regulated with 4 drams
powder H.P. machine ring
bullet Eleys 3¼ solid brass
case also regulated with
55 grains Cordite 365 grain
S.N. nickel bullet & Eley's
nitro case Sights 100·200·300 yards
← See below   ← See below

Memo 11883   29/8/02.
finally shot sights finished
& blacked &c

Mem 14425 20.11.03.
Shot & readjusted with 65 grains
"Cordite" 365 gn S N nickel bullet
& Eley 3¼" Nitro case

*These entries in Holland &
Holland's records show the
minute attention paid to
describing every particular of a
gun or rifle. They also show the*

results of all the regulating at the Shooting Grounds that took place before the weapon was finally judged to be ready for delivery to the customer.

The Holland & Holland Collection

We know something about the type of guns which Harris Holland was making in 1855, from which date records are available, and the Holland & Holland factory has, over recent years, received a number of early Holland guns for repair; details of these are available, and there are some early Holland guns in the firm's collection.

Let the guns, though, speak for themselves as these are the best evidence of the kind of guns Holland was making in the early years.

A rare double-barrelled 4-bore wildfowling muzzle loading percussion gun by H. Holland. The gun is unnumbered but the 37" damascus barrels are engraved with the King Street address. The gun weighs 15lb 12oz and was used extensively on the 24th April 1985 at the Holland & Holland Shooting School as part of the sesquicentennial celebrations of the Company. The gun was loaded with 8 or 10 drams of powder and 4 oz of shot and was fired at clay pigeons. Provenance Saltmarsh Hall 1971 – **Right top.**

H. Holland 8-bore double percussion gun serial No. 592, 30" damascus barrels, with ramrod in pipes, inscribed: H. HOLLAND, 9 KING ST, HOLBORN, LONDON, platinum vents, bar-action locks, scroll-engraved, inscribed: H. HOLLAND. Straight hand stock, steel heelplate. Weight 7lbs 11ozs. Overall length 47". Made in 1862 for Capt. Turner – **Right below.**

12-bore H. Holland underlever hammer gun, serial No. 1849, 30" damascus barrels, back-action non-rebounding locks, scroll-engraved, inscribed: H. HOLLAND. Inscribed on barrels: H. HOLLAND, 98 NEW BOND STREET, LONDON, straight hand stock, steel heelplate. Weight 7lbs. Overall length 45½". June 16th 1871.

A .450-bore 3¼" black powder express double rifle by Holland and Holland, serial No. 11380, 28" barrels sighted 50/150 yds, leaves 200 yds and 250 yds, incribed: HOLLAND & HOLLAND, 98 NEW BOND ST, LONDON and WINNERS OF ALL THE 'FIELD' RIFLE TRIALS LONDON 1883. Back-action hammer rebounding locks with safety bolts, and top-lever, all scroll-engraved. Action engraved: CHARGE 4 DRAMS CASE 3¼ INCHES and on lockplates: HOLLAND & HOLLAND. Pistol hand stock, with steel grip cap, cheekpiece and horn heelplate, Anson forend. Weight 8lbs 7ozs. Overall length 45½". Made 1887. (This weapon is in its original case. It appears to have been little used, and retains almost all the original action colours, blueing, etc.)

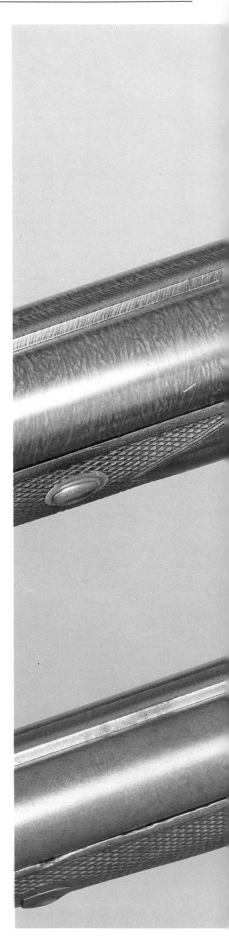

Those interested in records of the early guns will find in Appendix II a commentary on the records and gun numbers, going through to the 1870s, and then beyond as the firm's records became more sophisticated.

16-bore H. Holland gun, serial No. 2209, back-action non-rebounding locks, inscribed: H. HOLLAND, Needham's patent action, all scroll-engraved. 30″ damascus barrels, inscribed: H. HOLLAND, 98 NEW BOND STREET, LONDON, straight hand stock, horn buttplate, snap forend. Weight 6lbs 2ozs. Overall length 46½″. Made in 1872. (This particular patent of Needham involved a side-lever opening which lifted the locks to half-cock when the lever is depressed to open the gun, allowing the strikers to withdraw from the breech face).

A 4-bore single-barrelled gun by Holland and Holland, serial No. 4786, underlever action, non-rebounding lock inscribed: HOLLAND & HOLLAND, scroll-engraved. 42″ damascus barrel, inscribed amid scrollwork: HOLLAND & HOLLAND, 98 NEW BOND ST, LONDON. Straight hand stock, bolted forend. Weight 12lbs 10ozs. Overall length 60½. Made for Mr. Pratt, January 18th 1878.

A 28-bore Holland and Holland single-barrelled gun, serial No. 5806, top-lever, back-action rebounding hammer lock, the lockplate inscribed: HOLLAND & HOLLAND, the action and lock etc., border-engraved. 30¼″ damascus barrel, inscribed: HOLLAND & HOLLAND, 98 NEW BOND STREET, LONDON. Pistol hand stock with steel grip cap, bolted forend. Weight 3lbs 13ozs. Overall length: 46″, 1879.

H. Holland percussion spur-hammer transitional revolving rifle, 23″ damascus barrel, approximately 400-bore. Pistol hand stock with steel grip cap and steel heelplate, buffalo-horn grip for front hand. Inscribed: H. HOLLAND, 9 KING ST., HOLBORN. No serial number can be found on this weapon. Weight 5lbs 2ozs, Overall length 42″ – **Below.**

No. 1 of a pair of rare 4-bore black powder Hammer Rifles by Holland & Holland, Nos. 8333/4, made for His Highness The Nizam of Hyderabad in 1885. Each rifle weighs 22lb; the damascus barrels being 24″ long. The stock is inset with a gold oval engraved with The Nizam's coat of arms – **Above.**

A 20-bore Holland and Holland gun, serial No. 6106, top-lever back-action sidelock hammerless non-ejector gun, top safety, Scott's patent 'Climax' action. Scroll-engraving, locks inscribed: HOLLAND & HOLLAND, action inscribed: CLIMAX SAFETY HAMMERLESS. 28″ damascus barrels, inscribed: HOLLAND & HOLLAND, 98 NEW BOND ST, LONDON. Straight hand stock with recoil pad, Deeley forend. Weight 5lbs 9ozs. Overall length 44½″. Made for Mr. Gregory, May 29th 1880.

A .500 Holland and Holland black powder express double rifle serial No. 6423, back-action hammer locks, underlever self-cocking action, the locks inscribed: HOLLAND & HOLLAND, the action inscribed: CHARGE 4¼ DRAMS CASE 3 INCHES. Scroll engraving on action, locks etc. 28″ steel barrels, dolls-head extension, sighted 150, 200 and 250 yards. Pistol hand stock, steel grip cap, cheekpiece, horn buttplate. Bolted forend. Weight 7lbs 15ozs. Overall length 44″. Made for Mr. Woodville, January 31st 1881. This rifle was built on Perkes's Patent.

A 16-bore Holland and Holland 'Climax' gun, serial No. 11555, back-action hammerless non-ejector top-lever, top-safety, the locks inscribed: HOLLAND & HOLLAND, the action inscribed: CLIMAX–HAMMERLESS. Deeley forend, 30″ steel barrels inscribed: HOLLAND & HOLLAND, 98 NEW BOND STREET, LONDON, WINNERS OF ALL THE 'FIELD' RIFLE TRIALS 1883. Straight hand stock, rubber pad, leather covered cheekpiece. Weight 6lbs 1ozs. Overall length 47″

A .380-bore double-barrelled rook rifle by H. Holland, serial No. 2849. Back-action sidelever non-rebounding locks, inscribed: H. HOLLAND, action, locks, hammers, etc. all scroll-engraved. 27″ damascus barrels sighted for 50 and 100 yards, matted rib, inscribed: H. HOLLAND, 98 NEW BOND ST, LONDON. Pistol hand stock with horn grip cap, steel buttplate, bolted forend. Weight 6lbs 13ozs, overall length 44″. This rifle was made in 1874 for Henry William George, Marquis of Anglesey, Earl of Uxbridge, M.P. (1821–1880). It is in practically mint condition, retaining nearly all original finish, and would appear to have been scarcely used – **Top**.

A fine quality .360-bore No. 2 Rook Rifle by Holland & Holland No. 19508 fitted with an extra barrel chambered for the .360 Express cartridge, from the Armoury of His Highness The Nizam of Hyderabad – **Top below.**

A .303 single-barrelled back-action hammer rifle by Holland & Holland, No. 19656, the forend is stocked to within five inches of the muzzle, but is still detachable. The octagonal barrel is engraved: WINNERS OF ALL THE FIELD RIFLE TRIALS LONDON and the rifle is fitted with its original telescopic sight. Made in 1897 for the Count Erdody, the original entry states that it was finally shot on 25th September 1897 with its telescopic sight at 500 yards – **Below top.**

A rare .577-bore black powder rifle built on the Braendlin Albini system by H. Holland with the address of 98 New Bond Street, the rifle is numbered 1289 which dates it approximately in the early 1870s – **Bottom.**

A Holland and Holland Scott's action Perkes's patent 'Climax' action combination gun and rifle serial No. 8189, Back-action hammerless sidelock-non-ejector, the locks inscribed: HOLLAND & HOLLAND, 98 NEW BOND ST. LONDON top-safety, extra side-safety lever on left lock, 28″ steel barrels, right barrel 20-bore left-barrel .450/400 2⅜″, inscribed: HOLLAND & HOLLAND, 98 NEW BOND STREET, LONDON, and WINNERS OF ALL THE 'FIELD' RIFLE TRIALS LONDON 1883. Pistol hand, horn grip cap, cheekpiece, horn buttplate. Weight 8lbs 3ozs. Overall length 45¾″. Made for Hugh Lowther, the Earl of Lonsdale, who was a highly renowned sportsman and intrepid big-game hunter, the originator of the Lonsdale belt in boxing. He was born in 1857, succeeded his brother to the title in 1882, and died in 1944.

Holland and Holland 8-bore 'Paradox' ball- and shotgun, serial No. 15131, inscribed: HOLLAND & HOLLAND, 98 NEW BOND STREET, LONDON, PARADOX FOSBERY PATENT, sighted 50 yds, dolls head extension. Back-action rebounding locks, inscribed: HOLLAND & HOLLAND, underlever, long top strap, side clips, all scroll engraved, the action inscribed: CHARGE 8 TO 10 DRAMS CASE 3½ INCHES Pistol hand stock, steel grip cap, cheekpiece, recoil pad, loops for sling, lever forend. Weight 15lbs 10ozs. Overall length 43″. For further details concerning Fosbery's patent and 'Paradox' guns, see p. 43. Made in 1892.

One of a pair of 10-bore dual system Howdah guns Nos. 5031/2 by Holland & Holland, made in 1878, the 16″ barrels fitted with dual extractors for either pinfire or centre fire cartridges. Kindly donated to the Holland & Holland collection by J. Roberts & Son, Provenance H. H. Maharaja of Jodhpur – **Top**.

12-bore Holland & Holland Perkes's patent gun No. 4678, side-lever, self-cocking action, back-action rebounding locks, inscribed: HOLLAND & HOLLAND, 98 NEW BOND ST. LONDON, scroll-engraved, 30″ damascus barrels, straight hand stock, horn buttplate patent forend catch. Weight 6lbs 9ozs. Overall length 46½″. 18th October 1877 – **Below**.

A .577-bore Holland & Holland black powder double rifle, serial No. 14651. 26″ barrels, sighted 150 yds, leaves 200 yds, and 250 yds, with dolls' head extension. Back-action rebounding locks, inscribed: HOLLAND & HOLLAND. Underlever, long top strap, all scroll engraved. Action inscribed: CHARGE 6 DRAMS, CASE 3 INCHES. Pistol hand stock, horn grip cap, cheekpiece, rubber recoil pad, loops for sling, lever forend. Weight 11lbs 4ozs. Overall length 43″. Made in 1892.

A set of three Holland and Holland hammer ejector weapons being respectively a 12-bore 'Paradox', a .375 Express double rifle and a 12-bore game gun. This superbly engraved set was made in 1903 for H.H. the Maharaja of Kolhapur, whose crest appears on the lockplates. (Shahu Chatrapati – Maharaja of Kolhapur GCVO, GCIE, GCSI, ruled 1884–1922. He attended the coronation of King Edward VII in 1902, when he was invested with the G.C.V.O. In 1909 he received entitlement to a 21 gun salute. His only daughter married the Maharajah of Dewas Senior. Her son later became Maharajah of Dewas Senior, and inherited Kolhapur in 1947.)

The details of each weapon are as follows:

A 12-bore Holland and Holland 'Paradox' gun serial No. 15629, bar-action sidelock ejector rebounding hammers, top lever, long top strap, flat-sided hammers, De-luxe scroll engraving, carved fences, with the Kolhapur crest on the bar. The lockplates are inscribed: HOLLAND & HOLLAND, 30″ steel barrels with 'Paradox' rifled chokes, inscribed on barrels: HOLLAND & HOLLAND, NEW BOND STREET, LONDON and 'PARADOX' FOSBERY PATENT, and on rib: MODEL DE LUXE. Folding leaf sights for 50 yds and 100 yds. Half-pistol stock with rubber recoil pad. Anson forend. A silver plate measuring 3¾″ × 2½″ is let into the right side of the stock. Unfortunately the inscription has been removed. Weight 7lbs 8ozs. Overall length 45″.

A 12-bore Holland and Holland hammer ejector game gun, serial No. 23259, bar-action sidelock ejector, rebounding hammer locks, inscribed: HOLLAND & HOLLAND, engraved en suite with 15629 and 17766. Top lever 30″, steel barrels inscribed on barrels: HOLLAND & HOLLAND, 98 NEW BOND ST, LONDON, and on rib: MODEL DE LUXE. Straight hand stock, horn plate Anson forend. Weight 6lbs 8ozs. Overall length 47″.

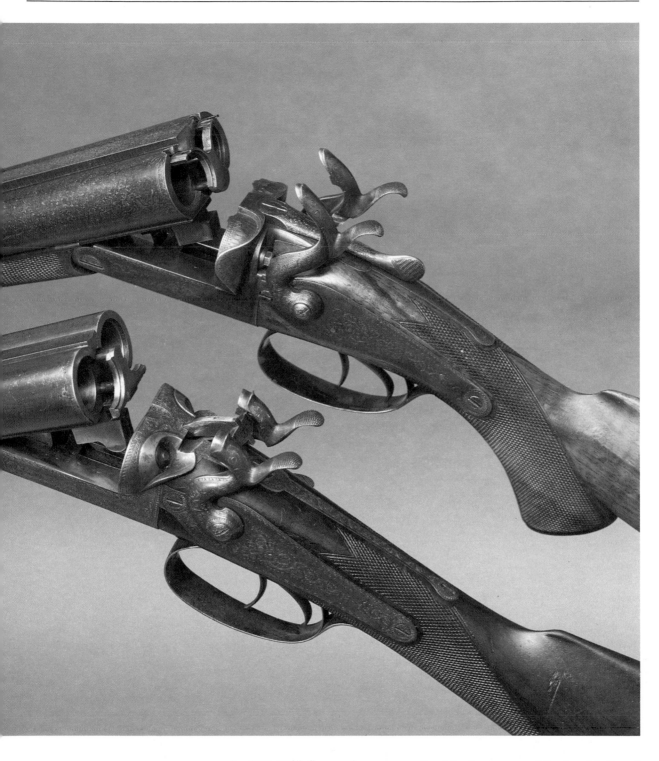

A .375-2½″ flanged express double hammer rifle by Holland and Holland, back-action sidelock ejector, serial No. 17766, rebounding hammer locks inscribed: HOLLAND & HOLLAND, engraved en suite with 15629. Top lever, long top strap, flat-sided hammers, 26″ barrels sighted 100 yds with telescope mounts for detachable telescope (which is now missing). Inscribed on Barrels: HOLLAND & HOLLAND, 98 NEW BOND ST, LONDON and WINNERS OF ALL THE 'FIELD' RIFLE TRIALS LONDON, and on rib: MODEL DE LUXE. Pistol hand stock, engraved cap box, cheekpiece, horn heelplate, loops for sling, Anson fore-part. Weight 9lbs 9ozs. Overall length 42½″.

A 10-bore Holland and Holland 'Paradox' gun, back-action sidelock hammerless ejector serial No. 15905, hinged front trigger. Detachable locks inscribed: HOLLAND & HOLLAND, the action inscribed on base: 10 BORE CHARGE 55 GRAINS REVOLVER CORDITE BRASS CASE 2⅞. Action, locks etc. scroll engraved. Top lever, bolted top-safety, long top strap, 27″ steel barrels with 'Paradox' rifling in chokes, sighted for 100 yds, the rearsight with ivory blade affixed, flip-up moon foresight, barrels inscribed: HOLLAND & HOLLAND, 98 NEW BOND ST, LONDON and 'NITRO-PARADOX'. Pistol hand stock with engraved cap box, cheekpiece, rubber recoil pad, gold oval, lever forend. Weight 13lbs 4ozs. Overall length 44½″.

A .250-bore single-barrelled rook rifle by Holland and Holland, serial No. 18663, boxlock hammerless ejector, top-safety, inscribed on action: HOLLAND & HOLLAND, all scroll engraved. 26″ octagonal barrel with folding leaf sights 50 yds and 100 yds. Flip-up Lyman aperture sight on action tang, flip-up foresight for aperture sight or V-sight, barrel inscribed: HOLLAND & HOLLAND, 98 NEW BOND ST, LONDON and WINNERS OF ALL THE 'FIELD' RIFLE TRIALS 250 SEMI SMOOTH BORE. Pistol hand stock with engraved steel grip cap, cheekpiece, steel heelplate, snap-on forend with horn forend tip. Weight 5lbs 9ozs. Overall length 42½″.

A 10-bore double-barrelled hammer rifle by Holland & Holland No 8266, gold inlayed and made for HH The Nizam of Hyderabad in 1884. This rifle is in pristine unfired condition.

'The perfect article produced in London'

The London and Birmingham Gun Trade

Sir Ralph Payne-Gallwey, a leading shot of his day.

'Many a shooter orders a new gun without ever seeing it, and then grumbles because he cannot kill with it, often blaming the gun, which is probably as excellent one, *but* a misfit. A man may just as well write for a new coat to a firm he has never dealt with, give the tailor no idea of his breadth or height, and expect the garment, when it arrives, to rival in comfort a masterpiece by a perfect cutter.

'London gunmakers undoubtedly have an immense advantage over those in provincial towns. Every sportsman visits or passes through London, and then has the opportunity of trying a gun, both in its rough state and in its finished one, at a "shooting school" . . . and as a rule, that "monstrous horrendum" a ready-made, reach-me-down Birmingham gun, is fit for neither man, nor bird, nor beast, and is a mere unwieldy log of iron and wood when compared to the perfect article produced in London.'

So wrote Sir Ralph Payne-Gallwey, Bart, in 1896. Sir Ralph was one of the leading shots of his day, and had a number of guns from Holland & Holland including the remarkable double-breech-loading flint gun. As we have seen, the original manufacturing head, Mr Harris J. Holland, had apprenticed Henry W. Holland, his nephew, in 1860, at the age of 15, and at the time Sir Ralph was writing, Henry Holland was very much in charge of producing 'the perfect article' in London. Up to his death in 1930, he continued to superintend the detail of manufacture, as we shall see in a later chapter.

The distinction drawn by Sir Ralph between the London and the Birmingham gunmakers was not one based on a snobbish preference for London, but it certainly gave rise to considerable ill-feeling, even more so when he extended it to cover all guns held in stock, that is, not hand-made for their owner.

How strong were the Birmingham and London gunmakers respectively in the early nineteenth century, and what was the reason for the comparative decline of the Midlands manufacturers? Fortunately, two historians, De Witt Bailey and Douglas A. Nie, have investigated the position of the gunmakers *outside* London, with remarkable clarity.* They point out the

---

English Gunmakers. The Birmingham and Provincial Gun Trade in the 18th and 19th centuries. Arms and Armour Press, 1978.

difficulty of defining a 'gun' when one is looking at the sporting gun of an aristocratic user at one end of the scale, while at the other there was comparative rubbish made for the African slave-trade and for barter with the native populations, in exchange for local products and raw material. These 'slave' guns were being produced by the million in Birmingham. In addition, there were the guns of the military.

We are concerned here with the category of guns made by Holland in London, where the historians say there was 'sharp competition to gain the custom of wealthy and prestigious clients'. Gunmakers in the metropolis were always striving for new features, innovations in mechanism, decoration, even sometimes in basic form. This state of affairs did not exist outside of London, where the mass producers of Birmingham produced to staid patterns which had achieved commercial success in the past with their export customers, and also made guns for the provincial retailers as close as possible to those patterns for the sake of cheapness and ease of manufacture. Hence a gun styled on a London design of the 1820s could easily have been marketed in the provinces in the 1850s. There was also, for Birmingham and provincial makers, an irresistible urge to sign one of their guns made in "London".'

Furthermore, at least one of the London gunmakers is said to have 'got the whole of his guns from Birmingham', these being 'fraudulently sold as the work of a London salesman, even if that salesman had never built a gun or made a part of a gun in his life'.

Shooting in London. The story goes that when the then Duke of Westminster was developing Belgrave Square, he received complaints that he was putting paid to the best duck flighting within easy reach of the City of London.

We must remember two things. First, Birmingham, now a city, had been a village of many manufacturers from medieval days, because of its favourable location near to iron ore and coal deposits. Well before the close of the seventeenth century there was a flourishing trade in guns there – they supplied the Parliamentary armies of Cromwell in the 1640s. Later in the century, Birmingham began supplying arms for the slave trade, and by the beginning of the eighteenth century, its manufacturers were also producing arms for the military, as well as components for the London arms trade. 'The production of sporting arms for the home market grew rapidly during the first half of the eighteenth century and more rapidly thereafter when both London and the provincial trade found it more economical to purchase either completed arms or the components from Birmingham.' By 1830 there was only one tube-maker remaining in London – the supplies came from Birmingham.

This is the second point made by the historians, that Birmingham was in large measure a major source of component supplies. 'Gunmakers were in fact merchants, located strategically between the material men (who made locks, barrels, furniture and stocks) and the fabricators (who assembled the components into complete arms). "Gunmakers" actually possessed no shops of their own, but rather owned a warehouse, where completed arms were stored for delivery to their customers . . . The "gunmaker" would travel about and obtain orders for various types of firearms . . . These contracts he would then sub-contract to the various fabricators . . . The man whose name appears on the outside of the finished gun was not the one who sat down in his shop and with various machines and hand tools shaped and completed the finished arm. The term "gunmakers" applied only to those who stocked and assembled the complete arm, made up from components obtained from those who worked in "Steelhouse Lane" – and at their peak, there may have been 15,000 of them.'

We are talking here of Birmingham in the 17th and 18th centuries, and the historians say that 'Birmingham's sudden rise in the gunmaking field did not go unnoticed or unchallenged by the old-established London gun trade. The well-organised Worshipful Company of Gunmakers in London had been founded around 1637, and its members now wanted to bring a halt to Birmingham's success, particularly as Birmingham guns were now being stamped 'London' to attract the better class of sportsman. In J. Morfitt's *Sketch of Birmingham* of 1805 we read

'Be it known unto all men . . . that guns with the best stub and twisted barrels, eclipsing the formerly famous barrels of Spain, the best skeleton locks, the best patented breeches, gold touch holes and are made here for one-half, nay one third of the price they bring in the metropolis; and yet a person unacquainted with the secret would suppose that Birmingham never produced a single fowling-piece, for our manufacturers have the policy to use the superscription of London'.

Earlier, in 1707, the Birmingham gunmakers had petitioned in the House of Commons against the London makers who had

Gun case labels of leading Edinburgh and Birmingham gunmakers.

the monopoly of proof. By 1815, it was the London gunmakers' turn to bring a bill into the House of Commons that would have required every manufacturer to place his real name on his product but 'such was the power of the Birmingham gun trade that they were able to quash the bill, pointing out that they supplied most of the components for the London makers.'

It is appropriate to pause here to ask the questions, was gunmaking an up-and-coming business in London in the 1830s, and how would one best go about making money in the trade? The famous Colonel Hawker, in his *Instructions to Young Sportsmen* first printed in 1814, has the following comments to add to what he claims was a 'hastily written' publication, in its 9th edition.

Colonel Hawker, perhaps the greatest shot of all time.

'Egg, that celebrated gunmaker, instead of "cutting up fat", as was expected, died like a man of genius; or, in other words, with his balance on the shady side of the book! The gunmakers, in short, still remain as I left them – like the frogs without a king; and, as before, complaining bitterly about the dullness of trade. But for this they have to thank their introduction of the detonating system, by which they got caught themselves in the very trap that was laid for their customers. When *flint*-guns were the order of the day, few sporting gentlemen of distinction ever thought of using anything but the gun of a first-rate maker, for the simple reason that – on the *goodness of the work* depended the *quickness in firing,* and consequently the *filling of the bag.* But, *nowadays,* every common fellow in a market-town can detonate an old musket, and make it shoot as quick as can be wished; insomuch that all scientific calculations in shooting, *at moderate distances,* are now so simplified, that we, every day, meet with jackanapes-apprentice-boys who can shoot flying, and knock down their eight birds out of ten. Formerly, shooting required *art and nerve* – now, for tolerable shooting (at all events for the use of *one* barrel) *nerve alone* is sufficient. Formerly, a first-rate gun was a *sine qua non*; now, the most that we can call it is a *desideratum*; since all guns are now made to fire with nearly equal velocity. Still, however, fortunately for the leading gunmakers, there are yet left many requisites which induce good sportsmen, though a much smaller number than formerly, to go to the heads of the trade: viz. I. soundness and perfect safety in guns; 2. the barrels being correctly put together for accurate shooting; 3. the elevation being mathematically true, and *raised strictly in proportion to the length of barrel*; and 4. the stock being properly cast off to the eye, and well fitted to the *hand* and shoulder. I say nothing of the balance, because any good carpenter, with some lead and a centre-bit, can regulate this to the shooter's fancy.

'Who is now to be called the leading gunmaker I hardly know; and there are so many competitors for the title, that it would be an unthankful office to name any one in particular . . . let me observe, as before, in answer to those who deprecate the idea of giving a good price for a gun, that the workmen employed by the first makers require wage *and indulgence,* in proportion to their skill in the respective branches of the business; and it thereby becomes necessary to charge for the guns accordingly.

'Many wiseacres abuse all the heads of the trade, and swear that they can *always get the best of guns, at a quarter the price, from Birmingham!* This may be, provided a person has such good judgement, or interest there, as to get *picked workmen for the whole process* of his order: but, in *general*, the immense business carried on at this place is for the *wholesale line*, and only requires to be *in the rough*; from which circumstance the workmen are not so much in the *habit of finishing* as those employed daily for *that purpose*. Moreover, if there is a first-rate and enterprising workman, he hears of the high wages, and contrives to get off to London.'

So, to answer the questions posed above, the trade was a 'dull' one and it was not unusual to buy guns wholesale from Birmingham and 'finish' them to a high standard (and a high price) in London.

One other aspect of the commercial gun trade is of particular significance – the import of fine guns from the continent, which continued through the 17th and 18th centuries, but virtually ended with the Napoleonic wars. 'Cut off from the continent, the London craftsmen began to create weapons which, in the field of sport, have never been surpassed, and are not yet superseded.'

Thus we can see that by the early nineteenth century, when Harris Holland (born 1805) was taking to the grouse moors, he might have used one of the better Birmingham guns (William Bishop, agent to Westley Richards of Birmingham, set up shop at 170 Bond Street in 1815) but he would undoubtedly have set his sights on acquiring a gun from the famous Joseph Manton, who had premises in Oxford Street.

Why did the Birmingham gunmakers let the quality trade slip from their grasp? The historians say that 'it was a combination of external changes over which they had no control and (their) internal inability or (un)willingness to adapt to changing (external) conditions'. A familiar comment, one might say, still to be found today in a political speech or *Economist* article commenting on the decline of British industry. The external factors were, in brief, the British government takeover of the East India Company; the formation of American factories to supply arms for the American Civil War which became the nucleus of an American arms industry; and the success of the continental factories (mainly Liège) where costs were lower. Internally, there was a tendency to favour larger groupings, culminating in the formation in 1860 of the London Armoury Co., and a year later, the Birmingham Small Arms Co. Ltd. (BSA) which introduced the factory system into what had been essentially a small craft industry.

Thus, by 1835, when Harris Holland set up shop, the keenly innovative gunmakers of London were establishing themselves as the leading suppliers of sporting guns to the gentry. This was a period of great development in improved detonating systems for guns, rifles and pistols. To understand their success we must also understand, as the historians tell us, that 'Firearms are, first and foremost, social instruments, and therefore historical objects. They reflect fully . . . the attitudes and abilities, as well as the aspirations and ambition, of the society that created them.'

The Worshipful Company of Gunmakers plaque on their building near the Tower of London.

The provincial gunmakers were also strong throughout the nineteenth century, as is evident from the list Teasdale-Buckell published in 1900, which contains over 150 names outside London and Birmingham. A writer in 1883 tells us that in that year there were 101 makers in London 'of whom 65 may be considered *bona fide* dealers or makers, the rest being implement makers, stock-dealers or popgun manufacturers.' One hundred years later many of the most famous names had gone, and today the Yellow Pages list only ten.

The other interesting question, for the historian, is why many London gunmakers concentrated on the shotgun, whereas in America and on the continent what commanded the inventor's ingenuity was the rifle. The rifle was, of course, the weapon of war, and in America to this day rifle and pistol are the machines which symbolise manhood, the machines which a man uses to defend his home, as well as the traditional method of hunting down his daily food. The prototype American is, is he not, the Deerhunter? He rides across the vast plains, through the dark impenetrable forests, bringing down his quarry with a single bullet.

The British scene was very different, and the shotgun was the inevitable product of a country where the necessity of continual self-defence had long ago passed out of the folk memory. Moreover, the landscape was also different – small fields instead of vast plains, copses instead of forests, and the indigenous game rather more picturesque than wild. Your average 18th century or 19th century landowner, proudly surveying his property, had not seen a wild boar for years, and deer were scarce in most areas. Indeed, truly 'wild' mammals of any size had disappeared centuries before, and it was not until Samuel Baker set about telling his travellers' tales towards the end of the 19th century that the British discovered the delight of big game shooting. And then they had to go to East Africa to obtain the benefits, if they were rich enough to do so. For the average landowner, it was fur and feather, essentially domesticated wild life, which could be brought down best with the shotgun.

It was at this time that the very word 'sport' became quintessentially English, denoting the kind of person who does not take matters too seriously, and can be counted upon to give his quarry (even if it is only a rabbit) what he came to call a 'sporting' chance. Is it too far-fetched to see the shotgun, as contrasted with the rifle, as the very symbol of this 'sporting' attitude? Well, perhaps this is far-fetched, and the truth may be nearer to one writer's view that 'the enormous population of birds, hares and rabbits (which) proliferated on the bounty of agricultural crops' were the ideal target for the shotgun which with an effective range of pellets between forty and sixty yards, could easily 'harvest them for the table.'

The fact is that the London 'best' gun became one of the symbols of British craftsmanship in the second half of the 19th century, taking its place with other products of excellence, and that Henry Holland became one of the most respected of those gunmakers of London, working in metal to a concept called 'perfection' in which no allowance was made for tolerances and nothing less than the best was permitted. So it remains to this day.

'The Sportsman' became quintessentially English.

'The Field' Trials of 1883

The foundation of the fame of Holland & Holland was not only the shotgun but the double-barrelled rifle in many different forms and calibre. The rifle-making world was highly competitive – in London alone there were the retail premises of Rigby, Jeffery, Greener, Westley Richards, Purdey, Wilkes and Lancaster and in the provinces there were two famous makers, Gibbs of Bristol and Alexander Henry in Scotland. Every one of these was constantly introducing some innovation, be it to rifle or cartridge, and each proprietor would be telling the prospective purchaser that it would be quite foolish of him to bother with the weapons sold by his imitator in the shop round the corner. In his book *The Gun and Its Development* W. W. Greener implies that there is no other firm at the same level of business as his.

The muzzle loading era began to diminish in the 1870s as the centre fire metallic cartridge was being further developed and improved, not only by the gun companies, but by individuals involved in the shooting world and, of course, by the ammunition manufacturers. Hunters readily appreciated the advantages of using rifles in .577, .500, .450 calibres which were lighter and ballistically superior to 8-bore and 4-bore rifled guns and far more comfortable to carry and use. Hammerless rifles with steel barrels came on the scene; one of the first was by Woodward, who produced a hammerless sidelock called The Automatic. To the uninformed today this sounds like a magazine-fed automatic, but it was in fact a gun

The Field *organised the trials.*

or rifle which automatically cocked when the gun was opened – a completely new concept in the 1870s although the accepted thing today. By the early 1890s ammunition and gun mechanism had advanced to the stage where the automatic pistol was being developed. In a mere 20 years, therefore, guns had gone from muzzle-loading to automatics.

The year 1883 was a landmark for Hollands, with their unparalleled success in the trials organised by *The Field*. A writer of the time explains:

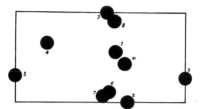

Holland's .450-bore at 100 yards.

'We do not mean to say that before that date Holland & Holland could not build a rifle as well as now; but what we do say is that the phenomenal success of their rifles at the trials in question set a higher standard for sportsmen and gunmakers alike than that which had satisfied both before. Of course it is a fact that most of the crack makers did not compete at those trials

and the account explains that

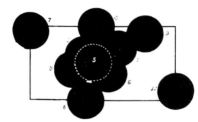

Holland's 4-bore at 50 yards.

Targets printed in The Field *reports were not to scale.*

'those who had most to lose were quite right in risking nothing. But Messrs Holland already held a high position as rifle-makers, and were doing a large business as makers of express and big game rifles, fitting out a great many of the more important expeditions to foreign countries.

'So it will be seen (he continues) that they had much to lose in case of failure, but they had so much confidence in the accuracy of their manufactures that they decided to run the risk and entered for the competitions. The results completely justified this confidence, as they won the whole of the ten series of trials, starting with the .295 rook rifles, and going up to 4-bore elephant rifles. The tests included nearly every class of sporting double rifle then made.'

One might say that Hollands went into the trials with both eyes open, because Mr Froome, who handled the matter, shot with both eyes open – a rare thing with a rifle. We are told that 'Mr Froome's method of shooting the rifle is exactly that which he uses for the shotgun . . . as regards position and getting the left hand well forward. He explains the quickness of aim is as necessary with the rifle as it is with the shotgun.' In another sense Hollands had their eyes open, because Mr Froome probably knew he could sweep the board. The firm not only had highly-skilled craftsmen building the rifles, but also the expert rifle regulators to undertake the difficult task of sighting the barrels to the required specifications.

To return to *The Field* trials, it appears that before they took place, a good deal of scepticism existed, especially amongst gunmakers, as to the correctness of the targets which were published in the sporting papers purporting to show the pattern of shots achieved at such trials. It was said that, after *The Field* trials, the majority of makers had to turn out work to an entirely new standard.

'These trials had this effect, that they taught sportsmen who had not had opportunity for the self study of rifle shooting what sort of a diagram to expect from a new rifle. It is a strange thing that so much inaccuracy had been hitherto put up with by sportsmen . . . The fact is that the manufacture of sporting rifles had settled down into a very few hands indeed; these were good ones, but there was no recognised standard of merit by which to compare.'

The Field trials provided this standard of merit, and Holland provided the pre-eminent standard to which others must try to aspire.

The trials were held at Putney in the first week of October 1883. The classes were for rook rifles, double .400, .450, .500 and .577 Express rifles, and for double 12-, 8- and 4-bore rifles. There were six competitors and Holland won every event, from rook rifle to 4-bore. Parts of the report published in *The Field* afterwards, read as follows:

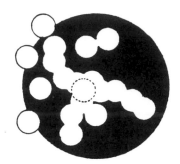

Holland's Rook rifle at 50 yards.

'Messrs. Holland & Holland can certainly congratulate themselves on possession of so competent an assistant in regulating and shooting their rifles. Mr. H. Holland, who personally designed the whole of the magnificent series of rifles, richly deserves the credit that attaches to their performance. The fact is that the construction of rifles and the proper adjustment of their charges requires long thought and careful trials and it it only by the combination of theory and practice such as is practised by the Bond Street firm that success can be achieved.'

So convincing a win was treated in a lightweight manner by some. Greener says, writing seven years later, 'To the gun trade, and to sportsmen in general, the trial cannot be said to have been fully satisfactory, nor to have produced the conclusive proofs that were expected'. He adds that for a rook rifle Holland's used a gun that was 'to all intents and purposes a gallery rifle, and although technically within the conditions, is not a weapon that would ever be taken out rook shooting'. He concludes, 'Holland were lucky in the possession of an

Gun trials and club contests were a feature of life in the 1880s.

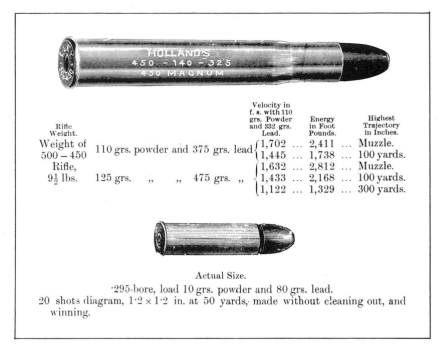

Rifle Weight.			Velocity in f. s. with 110 grs. Powder and 332 grs. Lead.	Energy in Foot Pounds.	Highest Trajectory in Inches.
Weight of 500 − 450 Rifle, 9½ lbs.	110 grs. powder and 375 grs. lead		1,702	2,411	Muzzle.
			1,445	1,738	100 yards.
	125 grs. „ „ 475 grs. „		1,632	2,812	Muzzle.
			1,433	2,168	100 yards.
			1,122	1,329	300 yards.

Actual Size.

·295-bore, load 10 grs. powder and 80 grs. lead.
20 shots diagram, 1·2 × 1·2 in. at 50 yards, made without cleaning out, and winning.

Detail of The Field *report on cartridges used in the trials.*

excellent shot and some good shooting rifles; but there was nothing made at the trial that was not previously known to exist, and there are doubtless many riflemakers who, before the trial and since, would guarantee the shooting of their rifles to equal the diagrams made. Indeed, we know for a fact that some have built rifles, guaranteed, and obtained better diagrams than any ever published. There have been unwanted delay and reticence in making known the diagrams actually made at the trial.' This last sentence in particular seems absurd, as they were published in full in *The Field* in October of the year in which they took place. One has to remember that Greener was a competitor of Hollands, and the fact is that, by the 1890s when he was writing, the effect of the trials had been to raise Holland & Holland head and shoulders above most of the competition, including his own firm.

Regrettably, none of the actual Holland & Holland rifles used in *The Field* competition was retained by the company for the museum. One can only assume that having achieved their purpose, they were put into stock for commercial realisation.

While Holland & Holland ended the last few years of the 19th century at the pinnacle of success in sporting rifle manufacture, their success did not stop there. Hardly into the 20th century, Holland & Holland introduced what was to become the most versatile and famous round of sporting rifle ammunition in the world – still included in most manufacturers' catalogues of today – and designated the .375 Holland & Holland.*

In 1904 the patent No. 27912 was granted to Henry Holland for a cartridge case having a ridge or belt at the rear of the case, in front of the usual flange. In this way there is a positive stop preventing the cartridge from entering too far into the chamber and setting up headspace.

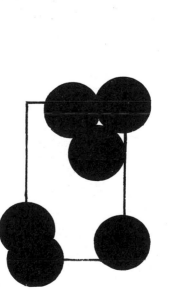

Holland's Paradox at 50 yards.

*In America known as the .375 H&H Magnum but probably few readers of U.S. rifle catalogues know what H&H stands for.

The first cartridge brought out by Holland & Holland on this patent was the .400/.375 Express, known as the .375 'Velopex' cartridge, after the type of bullet usually supplied. This cartridge was not a great success when used on big game, and therefore seven years later Holland & Holland brought out the .375 Magnum cartridge with a Belted Rimless case. This cartridge set the pace for medium calibre cartridges, and even today there are many who would claim that as an all-round cartridge it has never been bettered.

With all the facilities available to the company, it is not surprising that a great deal of experimention took place at the range with various powders, loads and bullets, particularly when a new cartridge was being produced. In the company's records is a hand-written book titled *Experiments* which comprises a series of memoranda and reports from the range

No. 27,912 A.D. 1904

Accepted, 26th Jan., 1905

Complete patent specification

"Improvements in Small Arms and in Cartridge Cases therefor."

I, HENRY WILLIAM HOLLAND, of 98, New Bond Street, in the County of Middlesex, Gunmaker, do hereby declare the nature of this invention and in what manner the same is to be performed to be particularly described and ascertained in and by the following statement:

This invention relates to cartridge cases especially for small arms.

The flange at the rear end of the cartridge with which the extractor engages was formerly usually made to project beyond but as this arrangement makes it difficult to pack the cartridges in a magazine this flange is now often made of the same diameter as the body and the bottle shape of cartridge alone is relied on as a stop but in such cases difficulty is often experienced in preventing the cartridge from entering too far into the bore of the gun and thus causing mis-fires.

According to this invention I form a small ridge just in advance of the groove for the extractor and I form a corresponding shoulder in the chamber of the gun. By these means I effectually prevent the cartridge from entering too far.

The drawing is a section to an enlarged scale of a cartridge made according to this invention. *a* is the body of the cartridge and *b* is the usual flange at its rear. *c* is the ridge forming the subject of the present invention.

Having now particularly described and ascertained the nature of my said invention and in what manner the same is to be performed, I declare that what I claim is:

Small arms and cartridges substantially as described and illustrated in the drawing.

Dated this 19th day of December 1904.

HENRY W. HOLLAND

Weight of
·577—·500
Rifle, 10¾ lbs.

The Field *report on the .577 cartridge performance.*

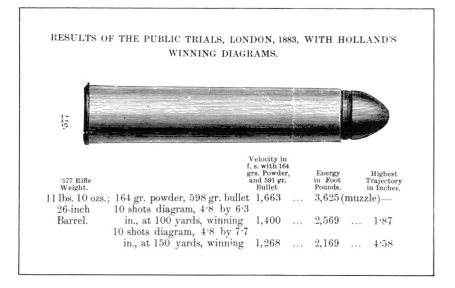

RESULTS OF THE PUBLIC TRIALS, LONDON, 1883, WITH HOLLAND'S
WINNING DIAGRAMS.

·577 Rifle Weight.		Velocity in f. s. with 164 grs. Powder, and 591 gr. Bullet		Energy in Foot Pounds.		Highest Trajectory in Inches.
11 lbs. 10 ozs.;	164 gr. powder, 598 gr. bullet	1,663	...	3,625 (muzzle)—		
26-inch	10 shots diagram, 4·8 by 6·3					
Barrel.	in., at 100 yards, winning	1,400	...	2,569	...	1·87
	10 shots diagram, 4·8 by 7·7					
	in., at 150 yards, winning	1,268	...	2,169	...	4·58

staff to the factory. Running from 1899 to 1905 it covers an important transitional period of change from Black Powder to Cordite and smokeless and nitro powders. The .375 Holland & Holland is well-covered: 30 pages of tests and reports plus a revealing letter to Kynoch's dated 19th November 1903 which although couched in most polite terms instructs Kynoch exactly how to load the .375 bore.

19th November 1903.
Instructions to Messrs Kynoch, re length overall of .375 bore Cordite cartridges.
"For magazine rifles the length is not to exceed 3.07" overall, and the velocity we wish you to keep to in our .375 ctg'es, is as near 2000 ft as can be obtained, but not to go below say 1950 ft. All cartridges for magazine rifles are to have boxes labelled with a red label "for magazine rifles."
For our double rifles the length is not of such great importance; the chief points are (1) the velocity should be as above (2) the pressure which we think you ought to be able to keep at about 14 tons.
The bullets we think you will find should not be inserted more than ½", it is desirable to keep them as near one length as possible, although ctgs even ⅛" longer would go into the chambers of double rifles, still as you know if the bullet is too near the end of the lead higher pressure *is set up in the barrel.*"
2nd December 1903, Instructed Mr Hillsden, that pressures may go to 15 tons, max.

The Paradox Gun

The Holland & Holland Paradox was also well covered in the *Experiments.* Invented by Colonel Fosbery and patented by the company in 1885, the Paradox was a gun rifled in the last 2 inches which enabled the user to fire bullet or shot. Colonel Fosbery was a highly inventive man who took out several patents relating to firearms and several others concerning other matters. The patent 7568 was intended to make a shotgun capable of being fired either with shot, without detriment to the pattern and performance, or a single projectile (either ball or bullet) with the accuracy of a rifle, without the extra weight involved in a rifle (the 12-bore rifles shot in *The Field* Rifle

Rifle Weight,
12 lbs.

20/·577

Trials of 1883 weighed 11½lb and 13½lb respectively: the weight of a 12-bore gun on Fosbery's patent was normally 7¼ to 7½lb). Holland & Holland took up the patent, and produced the weapon, which was named the 'Paradox'.

The guns were usually made in 12-bore, but 16-bore, 20-bore, 8-bore and 10-bore are also encountered. They were proved at the Proof House as for rifles, being tested with ball.

For the type of mixed shooting for which they were intended, they were the ideal compromise between the shotgun and the rifle, having the accuracy and power of a rifle of similar calibre, combined with the light weight of the shotgun. The advent of the Paradox gun more or less rendered obsolete the combination weapon with a shot barrel and a rifle barrel.

In 1886 the weapon was publicly tested at Holland & Holland's shooting grounds, and among those who reported the results of the trial was the magazine *Land and Water*, which wrote:

> At the invitation of Messrs. Holland of 98 New Bond Street, we attended a most remarkable trial of their new double-barrelled gun, the 'Paradox', at their range at Kensal Green. This gun is constructed to shoot any size shot, as well as bullets, out of the same chambers, and the plan devised for consummating this object they called the 'Paradox'. It consists merely of rifling about 2" at the muzzle, the whole of the remaining length of the barrels being smooth-bored.
>
> In handling weight, and appearance the gun is precisely like any ordinary double-barrelled shot gun, except that it is leaf-sighted up to 300 yds. Colonel Fosbery is the actual patentee, and Messrs Holland have developed and perfected

Sir Vikar-ul-Umva, Prime Minister of Hyderabad, killed three tigers with a 12-bore Paradox in 15 minutes.

Nitro "Paradox"
REGISTERED TRADE MARK.
Ball and Shot Gun

MADE IN 12, 16 AND 20 BORES.

Also in . . .

10 BORES FOR BIG GAME.

With Outside Hammer or Hammerless

With or without Half-Pistol Hand Stocks.

SMOKELESS PARADOX

12-Bore Cartridge with "Paradox" Bullet, full size.

With special bullets for expansion, or penetration as required.

The 'Paradox' gun enhanced Holland & Holland's reputation in 1886.

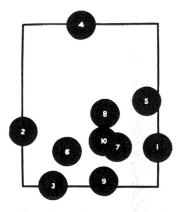

12-bore Paradox at 100 yards.

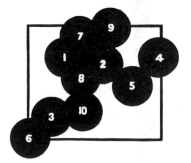

12-bore Paradox at 50 yards.

the invention. Amongst those present to witness the trials were Captain Ellice, of the Grenadier Guards, who attended on behalf of H.R.H. the Duke of Cambridge, Commander-in-Chief; Dr. Tristram, for Colonel Fosbery, and some few gentlemen representing the leading London sporting journals. The reason, we believe, why the military authorities attended the trial of this new weapon was to ascertain whether such as arm would be suitable for use in cases of riot or analogous operations, where the object would be rather the wounding of individuals by the use of shot than of killing them with bullets, while at the same time the weapon used should be equally reliable in case the more deadly missiles were necessary.

The 'Paradox' is made of various bores, but the weapon tried in the present instance was a 12-bore C.F., weighing 7lb 2ozs. We began operations about twelve o'clock; the sky was very cloudy, torrents of rain having fallen during the forenoon, and a few drops fell occasionally during the early part of the trials. A brisk wind blew across the range from left to right, and the conditions generally would not be considered favourable to accurate shooting. Mr Henry Holland conducted the trials, whilst W. Froome, who has for many years shot and regulated Messrs. Holland's rifles, and who is well known as a most expert marksman with sporting rifles, shot the gun in the first instance.

More details of the Paradox Gun will be found in the *Experiments* appendix. The heyday of the ball-and-shot gun really came to an end with the First World War, although Hollands continued to make Paradoxes until the 1950s.

❧❧ *4* ❧❧

'Two Wars and Two Depressions'

Holland & Holland 1905–1959

Business continued as usual right up to the eve of the war in August 1914, although it was said that some London gunmakers knew that a war was imminent because of the large number of German officers who visited London in preceeding months to place orders or collect guns. When war broke out, the changes were substantial. Several key employees left the factory to join the army, some going into the Royal Army Ordinance Corps as tradesmen. Although it was sad to lose experienced men, the immediate drop in orders meant that others were soon vulnerable. Purdey's history says that customers cut their orders by a quarter in 1915. Parkland was being ploughed up for food, and coverts were felled for much-needed timber. The order book at Holland's shows a similar picture. Lord Lonsdale, for example, who regularly bought guns, does not appear as taking a delivery after 1914. The shop book for the period shows comparatively few guns delivered in 1915, 1916 or 1917.

Yet it is surprising how many overseas orders were fulfilled. Business with the Austro-Hungarian Empire and the German Empire naturally ceased, and it was difficult to deliver guns to the Russians, although they were fighting with the Allies. Henry Holland did his best to collect money owing to the firm from such eminent shots as Prince Esterhazy. Orders from Italy, which had been a large purchaser of pigeon guns, also stopped, as did orders from Portugal and France. One of the last guns delivered in 1914 was for a Maharajah in India, but sporting activities in India and Africa were soon much reduced, and the order books, which had depended very much on big game hunting, began to look increasingly thin. But despite this, it is surprising how much trade still went on. Some 160 'Best' guns were delivered in 1915 to 1917 which compares very respectably with the rate of delivery today.

As early as 3rd September 1914, the Board met to discuss what to do, in light of 'the state of war now existing'. They decided that 'Having in mind the expected disorganising of business and the serious losses caused thereby, the directors present, Mr Holland, Mr Rayner and Mr Dawe, intimated their desire to accept a reduction in the amount of their fees – on the same basis as the staff and others had suggested, that is, a reduction of 25 per cent.' The factory had gone on to three-quarter time. Later, Colonel Holland, Henry's son, was to note

German Zeppelin airships flying over England were brought down by a Holland & Holland 12-bore shotgun. This arm, of which it is believed 200 were made and only two are known to survive, was designed by Holland & Holland and employed a special 'Duplex' (or two stage) choke bore. The weapon was actually made by

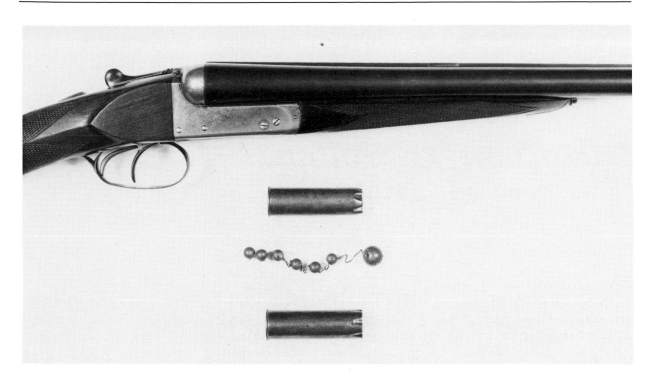

Webley and Scott in Birmingham, and was issued to Royal Naval Air Service units probably in 1914. Cartridges, which were produced in all-brass and paper case forms, were loaded with 'chain shot', one large ball and six small on a wire, and were intended to damage struts and fabric.

his pride in the fact that, throughout the war, Hollands did not pay a penny in dividends on the Ordinary Shares. 'My father would not countenance it,' he said.

The chairman turned his attention to the opportunities for war work, contacting the War Office about contracts for snipers' rifles, telescopic sights, and so on. The sniper is a twentieth century animal and although telescopic sights were used in the nineteenth century – for example during the Indian Mutiny in 1856 – it was not until the Great War that the sniper's art came of age, forced by desperate necessity. Britain was not entirely prepared for the static warfare of the trenches, as the Germans were quick to dominate No Man's Land and the forward zones by using snipers. By late 1914, the Germans had 20,000 sniping units in position, and the Duke of Ratibor collected thousands more sporting rifles which were also pressed into service. The disparity between the two forces became so severe that the British War Office even tried to obtain telescopic sights from Germany. Then the government turned to the gun trade, and issued contracts for supplying and fitting telescopes to rifles. Telescopes were scarce at first and up to July 1915, Hollands supplied and fitted only ten snipers' rifles; it was not until 1916 that Aldis and others began to supply telescopes in reasonable quantities.

Early in the war, armour-piercing ammunition was used to pierce the iron plate behind which the snipers were concealed, and by 1917 very successful ammunition of this kind had been developed. But before that, in September 1915, the British decided to 'bust' the enemy's armoured plate by ordering from Hollands and others 2000 large calibre express rifles which were commonly called 'elephant guns' because they made an almighty bang and revealed the sniper's position by their smoke and flame. They were not popular with their users. Hollands also made incendiary bullets, some of which were subcontracted out, and bomb slips.

Snipers came into their own in the 1914–18 war.

Throughout the war, and immediately afterwards, it had been assumed that Henry Holland (now well into his seventies) would be succeeded by his son Hal (H. R. Holland) – whose younger brother, Jack (J.E.D.) Holland, had never had any thought of going into the business, planning instead to make the army his career. Educated at Wellington, Jack was a 2nd lieutenant by the age of 21 and, arriving in South Africa in April 1901, where the Boer War was to end 12 months later, he saw active service with his regiment, the 7th Dragoons (known as 'The Black Horsemen'). For this and other actions he received the Queen's Medal with 5 clasps, was also promoted to lieutenant, and then in 1908 to captain in the regiment, as well as being adjutant to a Territorial Unit. During this time he made a name for himself not only as a sound regimental officer, but as a horseman and polo player. Like many of the officers he was probably on half-pay.

In 1914 Jack Holland went to France where he was awarded the MC and then in 1916, when he was a general staff officer, the DSO. He was also mentioned in despatches (by a curious coincidence the next entry in the Army Staff List at this time is Bill Payne-Gallwey). After the war, he changed regiments to the 5th Dragoon Guards, and in 1919 was listed Lieutenant Colonel.

However like many other survivors, Holland, who had been wounded twice, found the war too traumatic an experience to wish to continue in the army, and he resigned his commission soon after April 1921. He decided to take up farming and the breeding of thoroughbred horses, and the family moved to Ireland. There were three children, two daughters, Pamela and Shelagh, and a son, John, who went to live in Canada where he married the daughter of an industrialist Sir Adam Beck.

To return to Hal Holland, while his twin brother the Colonel was in France in the trenches, he appears to have been put in charge of the factory which was devoted to war work. On 27th December 1917, the Board passed a resolution that thanks 'be tendered to Mr H. R. Holland for the special work he has undertaken at the factory at Harrow Road, also that he has been asked to accept a cheque for 100 guineas as appreciation of this service.' And in 1918 the sum of 200 guineas was also tendered in appreciation of these services, as well as 100 guineas each to two other directors for special services in connection with war work.

In the early years of his directorship, from about 1905 to 1911, Hal Holland had not attended directors' meetings, which were mainly two man affairs between the Chairman and Mr W. A. Law (the latter retired from ill-health in 1912 and died soon after). Meanwhile Hal's health, which had given his father concern for some years, deteriorated. He spent periods in Switzerland, and it seems probable that he had tuberculosis. Henry Holland wrote to another member of the firm, 'Hal has to go for a long voyage and leaves for Australia very soon.' There are no records to explain why he was unable to take over more responsibilities in the business, but the long periods away must have been an attempt to restore him to health. Alas they did not succeed; from August 1920 Hal did not attend any directors' meetings, and he finally sent in a letter of resignation in June 1921. He died soon after.

For a time the firm continued under Henry's direction, with experienced members of the staff appointed to the Board to assist him – such as W. Mansfield and G. A. Pearce who became Directors in 1922. When Albert Madell went to Bond Street, in 1919, he found that a Mr Blomeley was dealing with nearly half the correspondence, as he continued to do for the next 30 years.

Henry Holland, despite the fact that he was approaching 80 years of age, had lost none of his business acumen, and in 1922 he negotiated the purchase of the freehold of Bond Street – 'for a mere song' says Madell.

His son Colonel Jack Holland, living in Ireland, still had no desire to enter the business, and he kept at a distance for several more years. However, in 1927, with his father's health worsening, he was finally persuaded to take his seat on the

Lieut. Holland (second left) during the Boer War.

Board. On 25th January 1930, Henry W. Holland, who had done so much for the company, died in his sleep aged 85. The new Chairman, E. G. Daw spoke at the Board Meeting of the firm's great loss. This was felt particularly strongly as the economy in general, and gun making in particular, were heading for a crisis. It was this year in which Colonel Holland gave up farming and took the chair of the company for the first time. In 1933, E. G. Daw, formerly the Chairman, retired in ill-health, with the Board resolving that 'after 40 years of faithful services, a grant be made to him of £500, payable by instalments, and that he be asked to continue as a director.' Colonel Holland had by now moved his family to Scotland, and for the next decade he regularly spent several days a week in London, and made it clear to all that he was now in charge of the firm.

Colonel Holland's desk is still in situ *in the factory.*

To return to 1931, the Board had to take account of the slackness of orders, and to find some ways of cutting expenses. Mr Mansfield, factory manager, was asked to put the men on three-quarters time and to make more cuts in wages. The following year the working week was reduced still further to 30 hours, and then there was another cut of 5 per cent in all fees, wages and salaries, and the dividend was reduced to 2½ per cent. By 10th August 1932 the Board 'resolved, owing to a lack of orders, to run the factory on a skeleton staff, dismissals of men to take place as they finish work on definite orders – but an allowance of 10/- per week was made to four workmen, while they should be out of employment and while the financial position of the company permits'. And an employee about to retire received a gratuity of £100 after 39 years of service.

The problems of the slump years of the 1930s shows clearly enough in the production figures which are for 'starts'. Guns would have been made for stock and in some cases finished several years later.

	Paradox	Best	Plain	Double Reflex	Total
1930	10	200	—	—	210
1931	—	100	100	50	250
1932	—	100	—	—	100
1933	—	—	100	100	200
1934	—	100	—	—	100
1935	—	100	100	—	200
1936	—	100	100	—	200
1937	—	200	100	—	300
1938	—	—	—	—	—
1939	—	100	100	100	300

The maximum number of 'starts' over this decade was thus 300 in any one year, with the average 176 and the lowest output 100, excluding 1938 when there appear to have been no 'starts'. Contrast this with 1910/11 when there were 500 'starts'. The depression was of course worldwide, and the American depression caused orders even from that source to dry up.

It was surprising that in 1932, despite the depression, the company managed to purchase 100 acres of rolling, wooded country at Northwood, Middlesex, for a new shooting school. It was a considerable improvement on the school in Wembley. The hilly terrain enabled it to be stocked with a great variety of sporting traps, with grouse-butts and partridge stands, and a 'walk-up' of various clays from concealed traps, so that there was good practice there both in and out of season. The purchase was doubly surprising in view of Colonel Holland's attitude to the school, which was at best ambivalent. It is said that he regarded it as a necessary evil, rather than a promotional asset of the greatest importance, which it later proved to be under other direction.

The answer to the conundrum was that the new Chairman, a shrewd man, realised that the firm's annual liability to pay £3,500 dividends on the Preference shares would be a great drain during the depression. He therefore decided to redeem the entire Preference capital of £70,000 by selling the Wembley

The Centenary dinner at the Connaught Rooms in London.

Park land to a builder for £1,000 an acre for house building and to purchase Northwood for £80 an acre. The balance for the share redemption was made up by selling War Bonds, part of the firm's investment.

In their history, Purdeys note that during the early 1930s in the factory, 'feeling was very bitter for these older man had no prospects of getting work outside as other gunmakers, in even worse straits, were cutting down on staff as well.' At Hollands there was also bitterness.

Colonel Holland did his best to drum up business by going on a visit to India (where according to his obituary he 'opened up a wide market') and by travelling extensively elsewhere. Reference has already been made to the 1935 celebrations of the firm's centenary. Speaking at the Connaught Rooms dinner, the Colonel said that he wanted to put on record that 'the relationship between employer and employees had always been of the happiest and there had been no friction amongst them. Adjustments had to be made from time to time, but they had accomplished them without any sort of friction whatever. They were particularly proud of the records of service of some of their employees.' He mentioned, in particular, S. Brown (finisher) apprenticed in 1879 and with 56 years service. Another eleven had joined in 1893 when the old factory was established, and they were still working for the firm in 1935.

What kind of man was the Chairman? Those social equals who got on well with him liked him well enough, but as an employer he was autocratic and could be difficult. A fellow director says, 'He was a fire-eater, and if there wasn't a fire he went out and got a box of matches.' And an employee says, 'Hollands in those days was run like a regiment, but there were no officers and no NCO's – we were all privates.' This last comment seems something of an exaggeration, as in the Colonel's absence Albert Madell acted as Regimental Sergeant Major, handling all the 'staff work'. The Chairman's dominant characteristic was the pursuit of excellence, and he was ruthless in dealing with those who, in his view, did not measure up to his standard – 'friction' was an inadequate word to describe what happened then.

By 1939, when he was 60, Colonel Holland was spending more time at the family house in Perthshire, from where he would travel by sleeper to London in order to be in the office for one or two days a week. However, he still not only retained the title of Chairman and Managing Director but did not slacken his hold on the firm's direction, and even after the war, when he was comparatively rarely in London, he still made it clear that it was he who made the decisions.

In the 1939–45 war years, Hollands once again took a large share of the military work available to the gunmakers. Despite the efforts of 1938, Britain was still not well-equipped to fight in 1939; to take one example, the War Office found it necessary at first to use 1914 sniper's rifles, removing the sights for mounting on more modern weapons.

A new No. 4 (T) sniping rifle was approved in February 1942, and from September of that year Hollands took up the conversion of virtually all the government's requirements for sniping, the rifles themselves being manufactured by Birmingham Small Arms (BSA). The following year, Hollands received a further contract and in 1945 there was a further order. In total well over 20,000 rifles were converted.

Other work included repairing and altering submachine guns and pistols, as well as rifles, and making and fitting silencers. Typical orders of the time are 'Manufacturing and fitting 100 sets of night sights to Colt Automatic Pistols and Sten Guns'; 'Making and fitting night sights to 6 Commando combines'; 'Fitting two silencers to two Mk V Sten Guns'; and 'Re-barrelling rifles for Vickers-Armstrongs Limited'. The firm also rough-bored propeller sleeves for de Havilland aircraft.

The factory thus kept busy during the war, despite building virtually no guns, but the records show that the low level of activity in the thirties further declined after 1945, and the average number of guns started in those years was 85 per annum. William McKelvey who worked in Bond Street from 1946 onwards, describes the firm in those post war days as a 'gentleman's shop supplying guns to gentlemen'. He would not use the word 'selling' to describe activities in an atmosphere that was more reminiscent of a club than a retail establishment; people who had not bought a gun for 20 years would drop in for a chat. Blomeley was still in charge of the correspondence, aided by Madell, and by Pearce on the technical side. Customers began to flock in again from overseas, from France, Italy, Austria, Portugal, India and the Far East and South America. One year, recalls McKelvey, the Australian team who came to Europe to shoot at St. Remo came over to England and every single member ordered a Holland & Holland rifle. Of course in the post-war years there were difficulties. Wood from France was non-existent, steel for the barrels was in short supply, and ammunition was difficult to obtain. The firm succeeded in buying up 1 million rounds of ex-Army cartridges, which were delivered to the workshop on the top floor of Bond Street, where they were converted by the staff.

Colonel Holland at the family house in Scotland.

Colonel Holland, who only visited Bond Street for a few days a month, occupied a small office at the back of the shop, and kept a stern military eye on the conduct of the business. If the carpet was an inch out of line, the staff would be called to put it back with precision, under his direction. He would view all the guns coming forward from the factory, and if he didn't like the look of one, he would have Jacobs (the factory manager) sent down to Bond Street to be hauled over the coals. His sense of discipline was not confined to the staff; one day he was entering the shop when he noticed a Rolls-Royce parked along the kerb in Bond Street outside. He told Madell to put a notice on the windscreen saying, 'Do not park your car outside my shop. Signed Col. J. E. D. Holland.' The owner, who was inside buying a gun, was not amused. Although he was only in the shop for a few days each month the Colonel kept in touch by telephone from Scotland, and when he was abroad in the winter, he would insist on a weekly letter from Madell.

In this way the firm continued through the 1950s, very little changed from the days of the 1930s, catering largely to the same kind of customers. 'For them,' says Mr McKelvey, 'there were three key dates in their lives – their wedding day, their first house, and their first Holland & Holland.' But life was beginning to change. The proportion of sales going to India and the Far East reduced, although Pearce had gone to represent Holland & Holland at the inauguration ceremonies to mark the foundation of the new nation of Pakistan, and had returned home with a useful batch of orders. Traditional markets were being replaced by more and more American customers.

And the Colonel's health deteriorated rapidly in the 1950s. He was suffering from emphesymia, contracted in the trenches in 1914–18 when his lungs were suffused with a mixture of poison gas and tobacco smoke. Already in 1954 he made an attempt to resign and hand over management to an outsider – but it came to nothing. By 1958, he was finding breathing very difficult, and moved down to London where he could have regular medical attention. He was not an easy man to talk to, even though he had softened with age, and two subjects were taboo – his family and its origins, and what would happen after his death. For instance, he had a great deal of help with the business during his last years from his son-in-law, Derek Mangnall, but they never discussed who would take over as Chairman. In fact, when he died in 1958, Colonel Holland was succeeded by Derek Mangnall, but, as will be seen, his was to be only a brief tenure.

5

'The Events of 1959'

Holland & Holland
1960-1990

The famous Bishop of Bond Street.

To get the full background to the events of 1959, we must go to Birmingham 150 years earlier.

Mr. William Westley Richards started his business there in 1812 and was extremely fortunate to be assisted in selling his rifles by the famous 'Bishop of Bond Street' who operated from No. 178, where he also sold jewellery. Bishop was described as 'a large roomy man, sitting in front of the white mantelpiece, his gouty leg up on a chair before him. Dressed from head to foot in the blackest of black, a huge white frill proceeding from his breast, and an enormous pair of shirt cuffs turned back over his coat sleeves, nearly up to his elbows. On his head, the hat, the celebrated tall, broad-brimmed hat, which no mortal eye had ever seen off his head. A truly right reverend and episcopal figure, and worthy of the only Bishop who had ever passed an Act through Parliament, as it was his wont to boast concerning the Dog Act, termed Bishop's Act.' According to Colonel Hawker, who calls him 'Uncle', he was the first man in London to 'serve gentlemen who want a good gun at a few hours' notice'. He comments that having a ready-made gun at a respectable shop was better than going to an inferior maker.

Westley Richards took out their first patent in 1821. They also worked with Brunel in perfecting the Whitworth rifle; assisted with the pattern of the Enfield rifle, and helped evolve the Lee-Enfield rifle. Indeed Colonel Hawker describes Westley Richards as 'Quite the star of Birmingham, with more business than ever'. Their Birmingham premises were at the further end of a narrow passage off the High Street, an unpretentious affair. In London, they had a shooting ground near the Welsh Harp, and must have been the only Birmingham makers to have such a school in London.

By the 1900s, Westley Richards's customers were said to include the Prince of Wales (later Edward VII), the Duke of Cambridge, and the Duke of Edinburgh, HRH Prince Christian, Marquis of Queensbury, Viscount Curzon, Lord Hood, and Earl of Essex, the Duke of Somerset, the Maharajah Cooch Behar, and many other men of distinction both in England and abroad.

This is no place to dwell on the history of the Westley Richards company, which, in 1946, on the death of the chairman, went into liquidation. It was bought up by a wealthy Birmingham businessman who appointed as Managing Director, Harry Rogers, then aged 24. On holiday in Kendal in 1947, Rogers met Malcolm Lyell then aged 25 and offered him the job of managing their shop in London, at 23 Conduit Street. Lyell knew so little about guns at that time, that he says he confused Westley Richards with the American firm Winchester. However, he took the job, which entailed not only learning a good deal about guns, but also about fishing tackle, which it was proposed to sell in the shop. Lyell says, 'I knew nothing about guns and nothing about merchandising and I didn't really know anything about fishing tackle – but I was keen on the two sports. So, I started on 1st January 1948 with a two-month course in their factory at Bournbrook, Birmingham. I stayed at a private hotel, where I met Tim Powell, then Joint General Manager of Mitchell & Butlers Breweries. I did a further month at the Westley Richards Birmingham shop in Bennetts Hill and in April I started at Conduit Street as manager.

'There was a basement filled with guns, rifles and goodness knows what – but one thing which I always remember was a certain baronet's grey top hat in a leather box, which he took away before Ascot and returned afterwards for another year's safekeeping.

'In those days a new "best" gun cost £240 and I think a double rifle £300. There were long discussions with Harry Rogers about whether we could up the price of the latter to £315!

'I soon realised the importance of second-hand gun and rifle dealing. In those days guns and rifles were generally taken back to their makers if the owners wished to sell – or else the owners advertised them, with a price, as a rule, in *The Field* or such like periodicals. And we had a basement full of weapons which had been there since the war. We gradually bought these from the owners. I became thrilled by double rifles – and what are now known as vintage rifles and guns. We started publishing lists of these and sending them abroad – mainly to America. In no time it seemed we built up a large mailing list and the weapons got snapped up.'

With the advantage of hindsight, it was Lyell's free-ranging mind, unlittered by conventional gun-trade tradition, which probably made his London shop such a success, as he adopted many original ideas, selling sporting pictures, sporting books and sporting gifts, as well as clothing, mainly waterproof shooting coats and over-trousers. But he admits that 'it was the second-hand weapon dealing which made the main profits. One worked on a 100 per cent mark-up on cost. About 1950 Knight Frank & Rutley started gun and fishing tackle auction sales – one a year I think, then two – where I attended my first auctions. I was very nervous! Among my first purchases was a double-barrel Joseph Manton – which turned out to be a fake. I think I paid £24 for it – and eventually got rid of it without a loss. We bought a large number of second-hand weapons from advertisements – but because people were wary about selling to a dealer I used to answer advertisements in assumed names including that of an aunt who had a good address in London. In 1954 the London gun trade was in the doldrums. Holland & Holland, for example, were advertising new Royals made to

Westley Richards's shop in High Street, Birmingham.

Mr Westley Richards aged 70.

Westley Richards shop in Conduit Street, London, from a photograph taken in the 1930s. Mr. A. J. Redfern, the manager, standing at the entrance.

measure for the "coming season". Meetings were held between the heads of many gun firms to discuss measures which might be taken to save their businesses. I remember attending them, but nothing really resulted: their businesses either folded or amalgamated.

'In 1954 I met Elliott Coyle, a prominent American gun collector, for the first time on his first visit to London, and we became life-long friends. He started to buy vintage weapons from us, and amassed a huge collection. It was about this time that I wrote to Harry Rogers and said I thought India would be a great source of second-hand weapons – but it was not until 1957 that I realised I had been right.

'At the end of 1955 Westley Richards told me they intended to close Conduit Street down, sell the lease of the building (it was a 999 year Corporation lease with more them 900 years to run), and try to get some other London gunmaker to be an agent for Westley Richards's new guns and rifles. Rogers told me afterwards that he had lost more than £30,000 since 1947 in the factory alone, and the London showroom was the only readily saleable asset. I can't remember whether he gave me a month or three months notice but I started at once looking for another job, probably outside gun-making.'

But Lyell's friends would not let him find another job and several proposed putting up the money for what would today be called a management buyout. He obtained a three-month stay of execution from Westley Richards and, by June 1956, seven of his friends had put up a total of £12,000 to put into a new business called Westley Richards (Agency) Company Ltd. Lyell recalls, 'Three people helped me through the first three months. One was Bob Moth of Hastings, a motor car dealer, but a gun dealer on the side. He let me have a number of guns on sale or return. The second person was Jamie Granville, a partner of Coutts with whom we now banked. He

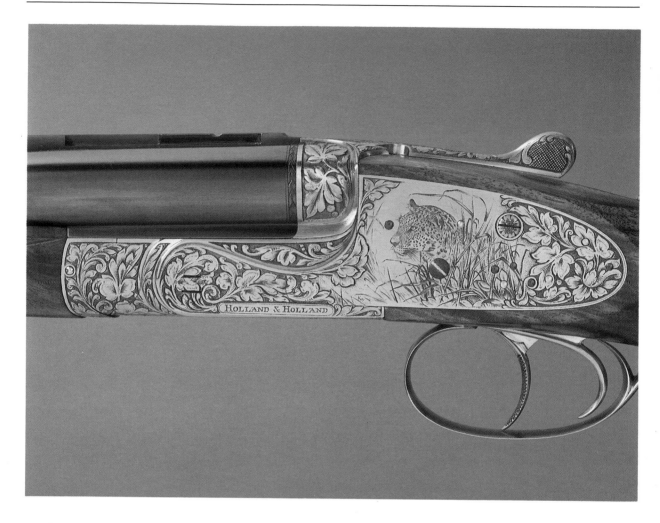

said, quite casually, that if I had to overdraw up to say £1,000 I was not to worry. (As far as I can remember I don't think we did.) The third helper was Knight, Frank & Rutley. They held a gun sale a few weeks after we started trading in which there were two pairs of guns which I knew I could sell easily – a pair of Purdey's in mint condition and a pair of Holland & Holland's also in mint condition. I asked the auctioneers whether they'd give me a month's credit – and they agreed. I bought both pairs of guns and sold them within a few weeks making £400 profit.

'By January 1957 things were on a sufficiently stable basis to allow me to go to India with my wife as the guests of the Maharaja of Indore (return air fares and all expenses paid by that wonderful man). After three weeks at his Winter Tiger Camp we went to Delhi and my thoughts of years before were proved right. The then Maharaja of Patiala was selling part of his armoury through an arms dealer in Delhi. I negotiated to buy some of the best Westley Richards guns and rifles subject to raising the money. A cable to Jamie Granville asking for £3,500 was answered immediately with a YES. This was to be the beginning of 21 years of weapon buying in India. Soon after we had returned home – via Persia where I spent three weeks on shikar – I learned that Farlows, the fishing tackle makers, and W. J. Jeffery, the gun and rifle makers, were both up for sale.

'Jeffery was a fairly easy purchase. The price we were paying

The illustrations on these pages are representative of the shotguns and rifles that Holland & Holland are making today.

LEFT: *A new .30-06 Royal de Luxe Double Rifle, the fences of which are deeply cut with oak leaf pattern, and the lock-plate engraved with a leopard.*

was ten pence halfpenny a share (old pence). That meant about £1,350 all told – the equivalent of our first year's profit at Westley Richards (Agency) Co. The deal was agreed between Mr. F. J. Pearce, the Chairman of Jeffery's who was retired and lived in the country. He came up for the day, had a Board meeting at their premises at 5B Pall Mall, and met me for lunch at the Westbury Hotel. I'd warned Albert their barman to provide Mr. Pearce with particularly potent dry martinis, which fortunately Mr. Pearce accepted when offered as pre-lunch cocktail. By about 3.00 p.m. Mr. Pearce agreed to the deal. Our accountant always says that the Jeffery shareholders fate rested upon those dry martinis and the fact that Mr. Pearce had to catch a 4.00 p.m. train at Paddington in order to get home to Devon in time to feed his cats. It proved a most satisfactory buy, and we were soon able to use up the very considerable tax losses! A more important point – we now owned a gunmaking name of our own. We also purchased Farlows but this was disposed of after the amalgamation with Holland & Holland.'

This may be a useful point to add a brief history of the W. J. Jeffery Company.

Gunmakers named Jeffery had businesses in Poole, Plymouth, Lymington, Dorchester and Farnham, all around the mid 19th century. One cannot help but wonder whether William J. Jeffery, later to found his own business in London, had any connection with these 'country' makers. All we know for certain is that he was born in 1857.

By the time he was 28, William had taken out a patent, No. 124335 for a device to allow for the internal inspection of gun barrels, several examples of which have survived. His address

BELOW: *A .577 Nitro Express Royal Model de Luxe Double-Barrelled rifle showing the distinctive features of the re-inforced action and long tang.*

at this time is given as 42 Great Castle Street, London.

A second patent was taken out jointly with E. Harrison in 1886. This was for a vernier and wind gauge sight adjuster. We know where William was living and the joint patent provides a clue as to where he might have been working. E. Harrison was the Harrison of the firm of Cogswell & Harrison and since William is described as a gun salesman in the patent, it is not unreasonable to assume that he was working for C & H as a salesman.

Another patent in the same year was taken out for a sight protector and it was not until 1897 that William obtained a further patent for a sight adjuster, this time giving his address as 60 Queen Victoria Street.

In 1890 the firm became Jeffery & Davies. In the following year the style was altered to W. J. Jeffery & Company and further premises were acquired at 13 King Street.

By 1910 the firm had showrooms at 13 King Street, St. James's and at 60 Queen Victoria Street. In addition the firm offered gun fitting at the South London Shooting Grounds and they had won prizes for sporting rifles at the Bisley meetings. At the turn of the century they occupied workshops at No. 1, Rose & Crown Yard, St. James's.

The range of guns and rifles offered, in what many would say was the Golden Age of Shooting, was quite remarkable. Their 'Best' London sidelock was £55 and their 1905 Model sidelock was £30.

The 'Best' Anson & Deeley patent gun could be had for £20 and for an extra £2 the gun could be fitted with Baker's single-trigger mechanism. The No. 4 A&D gun in 12-bore only was £5-10s-0d, black powder proof (Nitro proof cost a few shillings extra), and the firm offered a further range of A&D guns which could be had with either 2¾" or 3" chambers for pigeon and wildfowl. Similar guns were offered as hammer guns with top lever action and the lowest-priced hammer gun was the 1905 Model No. 5, a plain gun with Greener cross bolt at £4.

Single barrel hammer guns were available as were American 'machine made' single-hammer guns. For large game the company had a range of Ball & Shot 'Cape' guns, the right barrel chambered for either 12 or 16-bore shot cartridges and the left for the .577/.450 Martini.

There is little doubt that the firm was best known for its extremely comprehensive range of double rifles, the most impressive of which was the truly magnificent Jeffery double 600-bore. The rifle and cartridge was introduced by Jeffery in 1903 as a smokeless powder alternative to the massive 4 and 8 bore black powder rifles. The first 600-bore was actually built in 1901 and it was regulated for a charge of 120 grains of cordite and a 900 grain bullet; this monster weighed in at 12 lb.

Jeffery claimed that these rifles had a muzzle energy of 8,700 ft lb against the 7,000 ft lb of a 4 bore burning 14 drams of black powder. Jeffery advised using his push-forward snap action underlever ejector double rifle with 24" barrels. In 1910, made in best quality with doll's head extension, the .600 double rifle cost £65. A range of Mauser, Mannlicher and Mannlicher-Schoenauer sporting bolt action rifles was also available in various grades as was a range of single shot rifles built on the Farquharson type falling block action. These very desirable rifles could be had in all calibres from .600 in the 1904 model down to .22 rim-fire in the 1906 model.

The Company continued its work on sights and in 1900 they obtained a patent for a vertical post graticule for telescopic sights instead of the then fashionable 'cross hairs'. The last patent was for an aperture back sight attached to the breech bolt of the Mauser action and the Jeffery 'Patent Peep Sight' could be fitted to the Model 1908 Mauser rifle for 21 shillings.

The founder, William Jackman Jeffery, died in March 1909 and the direction of the company's affairs was taken over by his brother Charles.

The effect on the company of the First World War can be seen by the closure of the King Street premises and those at Rose & Crown Yard. In 1920, Charles Jeffery died and the direction of the company was entrusted to his nephew, Pierce Jeffery. Seven years later the company moved from Queen Victoria Street to 9 Golden Square, Regent Street, near Piccadilly Circus. By this time the price of the best sidelock had risen to £100 and an interesting 'Best' A&D ejector gun, the Model No. 5, was now £40. The range of guns and rifles on offer had not diminished, and the .600 Cordite Express was still being built on the push forward, under lever push forward action.

The range of cartridges associated with the name of Jeffery includes the following: .255 Rook, .280, .333 Flanged Nitro Express, .333 Rimless, .400 Jeffery, the .404 Jeffery, .450 No. 2 Nitro and the .475 No. 2 Nitro and, of course, the .600.

The effects of the Second World War reduced the business available for the company and their 1949 catalogue reflected the change in fortunes, not only of the company, but also of the country. On offer were three A&D action guns, Models No. 1, No. 2 and No. 3. The top of the range were some .404 magazine rifles built on the P.14 Enfield action for £75.

In 1955 a move was made to 5b Pall Mall and their catalogue included a sidelock as well as the three A&D action guns. Bolt action magazine rifles were still being built on the P.14 action and were now available in a wider range of calibres, .275, .30-'06 and .404 Magnum. The firm was saved from possible extinction by its purchase by Holland & Holland in 1960.

To return to the late 'fifties, Lyell's connection with Holland & Holland now began to materialise, although he had, over the years, met with several of their people at gunmakers' meetings. Lyell recalls: 'In May 1958 we were giving a reception at Conduit Street, and it was suggested we invited Derek Mangnall whom we knew had become chairman of Holland & Holland. Derek came, and that was the first time he and I met, although only briefly. Six months later he rang me up and asked me to lunch at the Cavalry Club. During our second cup of coffee he asked whether we would be interested in an amalgamation with Holland & Holland. I said, yes of course.'

In order to finance the purchase, which we should today call a reverse takeover, the Holland family took out of the sale the Bond Street premises and the shooting school and agreed a debenture of £10,000. Both sides agreed to acquire the lease of 13 Bruton Street. A new holding company was formed, eventually called Holland, Farlow and Lyell Limited.

On 3rd September 1959, *The Times* reported the position factually but the *Daily Telegraph*'s gossip column contained an item 'Gunmakers Unite' which gave the – misleading –

impression that Westley Richards of Birmingham had amalgamated with Hollands. It was a natural mistake to occur, and there was some confusion in the public's mind for several years to come. In 1963, a board meeting discussed this as one of the few problems that had arisen since the amalgamation, as customers were 'very confused as to which company they are dealing with'. In the event, the Board unanimously decided that it was desirable to create 'one image to customers' and so Holland & Holland it became again and so it has remained from that day.

Lyell recalls that 'Geoffrey Brooks was factory manager when the amalgamation took place. It presented a problem (not Geoffrey, but the factory). Little money had been spent on it during Colonel Holland's era. If a replacement machine was required, a second-hand one was bought. The machines in the machine shop were nearly all belt-driven. The craftsmen were all fairly old, although apprentices were taken on – but it was difficult to keep them. We did make a start on the personnel side by going to Eibar in Spain – the centre of the Spanish gunmaking industry – to recruit actioners and stockers for retraining to Holland & Holland standards. At first we housed them in the caretaker's flat in the factory but then we bought a house in Kilburn for them. Three of those men are still with us, and are totally assimilated into Holland & Holland after more than 20 years with the company.

'During those first five or six years after the amalgamation we sought to improve our manufacturing methods. John Batten, North American non-executive director, and his Chief Engineer Soren Sorensen at the Twin Disc Company in Racine, Wisconsin, were particularly helpful during visits to the US by Geoffrey Brooks, and various experimental engineers were invited. Highly experienced engineers from other firms were invited to see our factory operations. They were all amazed by the standards of craftsmanship – but not a great deal came of their reports. Perhaps, though, it did help Geoffrey Brooks for he was able to assimilate their thoughts and ideas. In addition, the Board agreed to commission a very helpful report from the Production Engineering Research Association (PERA) and also that Geoffrey Brooks and myself should go to the Continent and see the famous Fabrique Nationale factory at Liège, the Beretta factory in Brescia, as well as the A.Y.A. factory in Eibar. In addition Brooks visited Ferlach in Austria where sporting guns and rifles are made on similar lines to the British. All of this was very educational, and of great benefit to the company.

'Before the amalgamation it was agreed that both companies had the right to equal representation on the Board. It was never exercised. Also it was agreed that as Westley Richards (Agency) was supplying the Managing Director, Hollands

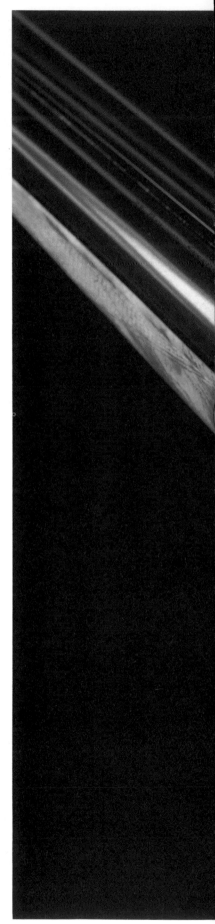

A 12-bore Model de Luxe with acanthus leaf engraving and deeply-carved fences.

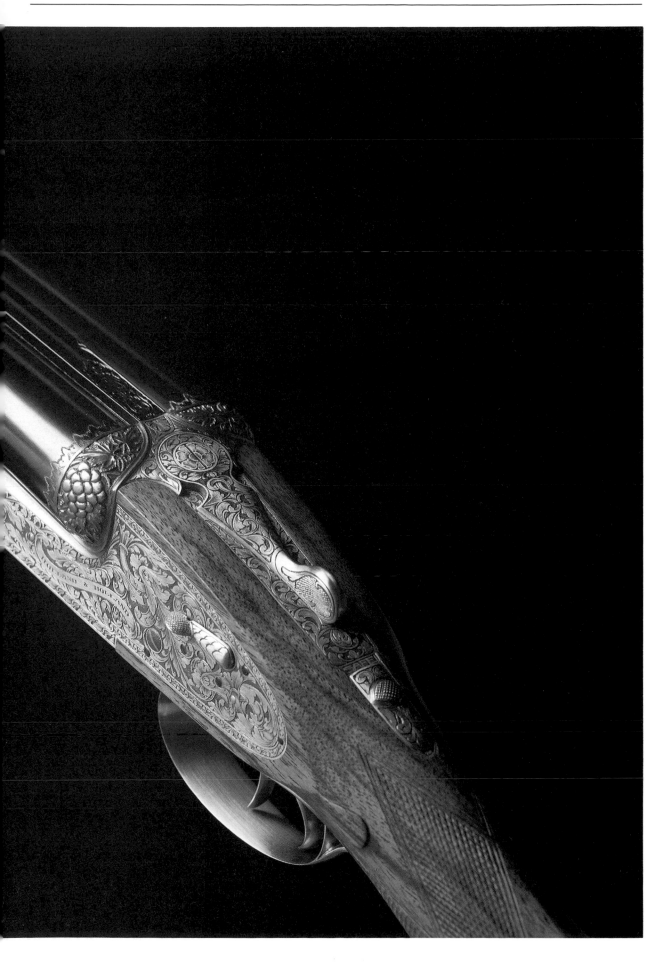

should supply the chairman for the first two years (Derek Mangnall) and that Adrian Hadden-Paton should be chairman for the following two years. At the end of the four years it was felt that the company would be so united that it wouldn't present a problem to elect a permanent chairman. So Adrian took over for his two years in 1962. But then before his two years was up Derek Mangnall retired from the Board because of pressure from other business interests and when Hadden-Paton's two year period was up it was Gavin Johnston (the Colonel's son-in-law) who quite spontaneously proposed that Adrian should become the permanent chairman – which role he carried out with tact and great dignity for exactly 20 years to 1982.

'Within 5 years the Holland family interest was reduced from approximately 50% to about 20% and other interests took over their shareholding. One of these was Jack Wynne Williams – Chairman of one of the leading advertising agencies in London – who was appointed a Director in 1966, and remained on the Board until his death in May 1977. Then Keith Showering took his place on the Board, until his sudden death at a Governor's meeting at the Bank of England in March 1982. It was a terrible blow not only to his family, but to Holland & Holland, and me in particular as I had come to know him so well and was looking forward to his becoming Chairman of the company in the years to come.

'In the late autumn of 1965, it had been decided that we must make a visit to the United States. Purdeys had been making yearly visits since soon after the end of the war. In 1965 our delivery dates for new guns had come down to less than two years, and we had some guns available for delivery between 9 to 14 months, so this was a good moment to expand markets. I don't think I ever worked so hard as I did in those months preparing for the eight week U.S. tour starting in April 1966. Acting on my golden rule that one must do everything on a bigger and better scale than one's competitors, I planned the

A Model de Luxe Magazine Rifle with buffalo horn forend tip, and gold inlay work on the magazine plate. The folding foresight protector is shown folded forward.

visit to include my wife Rosamunde and Norman Clarke, and set up so to speak a "mini" Holland & Holland shooting school at gun clubs or country clubs where they had clay pigeon facilities. Our friends in the various U.S. cities were unbelievably kind – first in helping to set up the facilities, and then publicising our visit, and giving parties to which they asked all their shooting friends and potential gun and rifle buyers. We never stayed in an hotel all the time we were there, and furthermore, I realised how much more cachet there would be if we added to the "circus" by having Trilok, our Indian servant, come out and join us – which he did.

'This visit led to Norman Clarke going out on his own in 1967 to New York for three weeks under the auspices of Abercrombie and Fitch at the Camp Fire Club. Earle Angstadt (President of Abercrombie & Fitch) had been tremendously impressed by the public relations value to his company – and of course this is an equally important reason from Holland & Holland's point of view too. In 1968 I put the show on the road again (but without, alas, Trilok). This time we started on the West Coast – Seattle, to San Francisco, and then down to Los Angeles. Then on to Texas, Houston and Dallas and from there to Atlanta where the Alfred Kennedys were so kind, and where we took more orders than anywhere else.

'I was a bit hesitant about that visit. Our delivery time was over 2½ years, and with the spate of orders which came in during the last of the 1960s and the beginning of the 1970s we have never gone out on a planned gun order promotional tour again. Instead we have had modest exhibitions at wildlife conventions in America and they too have been highly successful. In fact at one we bought a large number of English second-hand guns and had them shipped back to England for re-sale. The Holland & Holland tours by a shooting instructor have however been continued right up to the present time – and long may they continue. Our instructors have been wonderful ambassadors for the company.'

Another fine ambassador has been Jeremy Clowes who joined the company in 1966 and has travelled extensively in India, the United States, and the Middle East.

A major aim of Lyell's marketing strategy was to continue to attach great importance to second-hand sales. 'It was second-hand guns and rifles from which we made the profits in the Westley Richards (Agency) days 1956 to 1960. The same applied after the amalgamation in 1960, and it continued afterwards particularly because of the Indian Princes' armouries – especially when one was buying collections. My first purchase of a collection was in April 1954 when I heard that a new manager had been appointed at Dickson's in Edinburgh. He wanted to have a clear-out of his basement and so I phoned and asked whether I could have a look. I caught the night train to Edinburgh that evening and was on the doorstep in Frederick Street at 8.30 a.m. waiting for them to open. Downstairs, it was very dark because I think there was only one electric light bulb in a very large windowless room – it was a forerunner of things to come in India, only there one had the heat to contend with as well. I tried not to show my excitement when I saw the Aladdin's Cave! There were hundreds of vintage and antique guns in cases, as well as 20th century rifles – doubles, Farquharsons and so on. We did a deal that afternoon, and Elliott Coyle bought many of them a week or so later on his first visit to London.

'Whilst we bought modest collections after that in England – notably that of Lord Egerton of Tatton after his death – it was not until the Indian collections that we really became collection-buying minded, and these culminated in the largest of all – namely the Nizam's in 1974. But there was one other exceptional collection. This was that of the Kenya Police at Gilgil, north of Nairobi. We had known of its existence for some time but the crunch didn't come until after 11th December 1963 when Prince Philip and Jomo Kenyatta watched the Union Jack taken down and the new independent Kenyan flag go up. A month later the Kenyan army mutinied and President Kenyatta had the Scots Guards flown out to save his regime. He also ordered the weapons in Gilgil to be sent out of the country and the ammunition to be dumped in the Indian Ocean. A train took it all to the coast and a ship took the ammunition 30 miles out to sea and dropped it overboard and another ship took the weapons to Antwerp where they were put in bond in the docks. We spent three days there going though hundreds of cases of weapons – guns, rifles, pistols and revolvers. It was cold and damp and dreary in that bonded warehouse – but the excitement of finding so many rare Mauser rifles sent out to Charles Heyer in Nairobi fifty years before and inlaid in silver on the barrels with his name, together with many many more rare pieces, must have kept us going. I remember on my return to England in May saying to a colleague that I hoped we hadn't bought too many of these rifles. His reply was, "Mr Lyell, in a few years time we will be wishing we could buy another lot like that." He was right. Strangely enough we did buy a lot – at auction in early 1985 – of five of those beautiful Mauser rifles ex Gilgil. They cost us about £500 each then, action value only, as opposed to £10 or £15 each in 1964.

The shop at the new Bruton Street premises, although now selling a wide range of merchandise, still has the atmosphere of an old gun room. On the right Mr. W. McKelvey – Sales Director: on the left Mr. David Winks, an arms expert of international repute.

'When inflation "took off" in 1970 all new Holland & Holland weapon orders were on fixed price contracts and our order book at that time had extended to five year delivery. Whilst we had an inflation clause in our terms of contract the percentages by which we could increase the invoice price were quite inadequate. We discontinued firm quotations in 1973 just after I had taken orders from 5 people from Atlanta for 11 guns one Saturday morning. During the early 1970s we were therefore invoicing double gun and double rifle orders at prices which were giving us little or no profit. But fortunately for us the Indian Princes were under increasing pressure from the Indian Government to dispose of their armouries, and because of our very active purchasing of these arms we were able to make considerable profits on these weapons when they arrived in England. This helped to balance the low profits being made on new gun orders. Indeed in 1972 I spent a total of 4½ months of that year on three separate buying trips. Two visits a year had been normal. Fortunately, we had a very experienced sales and administrative staff at Bruton Street and I could leave for India at a moment's notice and be away for a month or two months at a time without much problem.'

In 1982, Tim Powell, who had been one of the trio instrumental in bringing Malcolm Lyell into his own business, when Westley Richards decided to sell up in 1956, succeeded Adrian Hadden-Paton as chairman. Two years later Roger Mitchell joined the company as Managing Director, thus allowing Malcolm Lyell, 25 years after the amalgamation, to devote more time to those areas which have played a key part in the development of the business including the building of overseas relations and the planning of special weapons.

Thus after 150 years, the company had a management team which had outlined guidelines for future development based on generations of skill and experience. In his Chairman's statement in 1985, Tim Powell summed up:

> 'For all that has been said about second-hand guns, it is on the skills of our production activities that the fame of this company will continue to depend. The London factory now has a sister plant at Birmingham, in the shape of W & C Scott (Gunmakers) Ltd whose origins go back to 1834. This additional unit of skilled craftsmanship provides a source of supply of quality boxlock guns, and a base for a new range of Holland & Holland guns in the future.'

A further acquisition completed in the 150th year took the form of a major part of the business of Rowland Ward (Knightsbridge) Ltd. This is predominantly the wildlife book trade. Rowland Ward has been an old-established name in the natural history business and taxidermy field for nearly 100 years.

Throughout much of the 155 years of its existence, Holland and Holland has been a private company but with a declining involvement of family interests, and with certain large 'outside' shareholders. Capital, as required, was financed from reserves, from borrowing and from customer deposits. In 1987 the management, under the new leadership of R. M. Mitchell, recommended to the Board that the time had come to raise substantial capital in order that

> 'a more expansionist strategy should be developed and implemented . . . Gunmaking should remain the core business but . . . a broader product and profit base (should) be developed, particularly in terms of high quality weapons for general use. The acquisition of W & C Scott's gunmaking facilities and skilled staff is seen as the springboard from which a broader product range of Holland & Holland weapons can be offered. At the same time, there are business development opportunities in the areas of retailing and shooting services which it is felt can be exploited.'

These quotations are taken from the prospectus issued in July 1987 which sought to finance this development and expansion by raising nearly £1 million net of expense. Under the guidance of the Managing Director and the new non-executive Chairman, Andrew Hugh Smith, Chairman of stockbrokers Capel Cure-Myers and soon to be Chairman of the International Stock Exchange, the proposed issue was successfully subscribed. In all, 450,000 shares at 10p were issued.

The prospectus noted that the company's revenue was in the following proportions: 32 per cent gun-making, 34 per cent bought-in guns, 18 per cent clothing and accessories, 6 per cent instruction and facilities. In 1987, exports accounted for very nearly half of income.

By 1989, the Chairman told shareholders: 'We have now come to the conclusion that our plans should be bolder than those we originally had in mind at the time of the share issue in 1987, and we have also concluded that these new plans should include proposals to change the organisational structure of the company.' The latter included a new retail division. 'It is now clear to us that successful merchandising operation would very substantially exceed that of the gunmaking and shooting services side of the business.'

In the latter connection, the company had already expanded its book business into other publishing areas such as video instructional films, and there was a useful side-line in picture sales. Premises to house the retail division were acquired at 31 Bruton Street, close to No. 33, which itself underwent extensive refurbishment during 1989 and 1990.

Further capital was invested to modernise the gunmaking division. The Birmingham workshops were equipped with computer-assisted design facilities and CNC machining centres were installed for component-making. This allowed raw components to be made to much closer tolerances than previously possible, enabling the gunsmiths to concentrate entirely on their true skills of hand fitting and finishing. The aim was to reduce the lead time on gun production to under two years.

If, in the words of the Chairman, even bolder plans were called for it would require further restructuring and this took place in June 1989 when, after having rejected a partial offer for the shares capital from a group of London businessmen, the board recommended a £10.8 million offer for the company from Sidelock Ltd, a subsidiary of the Chanel group. This valued the shares at £9 compared with the issue price of £2.25 when the public offer was made in August 1987.

Thus Holland & Holland returned to private ownership as a wholly-owned subsidiary of Chanel Limited.

Predictably, this seemingly unlikely acquisition prompted a certain amount of speculation within the gun world. However, Chanel were quick to give their assurance that the long-term development of gun-making – the 'core' business – would be uppermost in their plans. Holland & Holland would be managed quite seperately from Chanel's main activities and the existing Board of Directors continues to operate the company under the Chairmanship of Andrew Hugh Smith. This partnership with Chanel will, therefore, enable Holland &

Holland to retain its skills as a traditional British gunmaker.

So far as the Retailing Division is concerned, Chanel's acknowledged expertise will play an essential part in the continuing development of clothing, accessories and gifts.

The Queen at the Holland & Holland stand with the Duke of Wellington and the Chairman, Andrew Hugh Smith. The Game Fair, Stratfield Saye, 1989.

Making guns 'According to Instructions'

At the factory

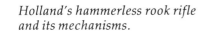

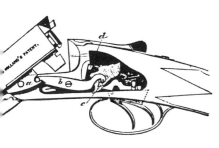

Holland's hammerless rook rifle and its mechanisms.

Royal hammerless gun and its lock.

Whether Harris Holland made, or only finished guns at No. 9 King Street, London, is not clear 150 years later. He and his wife (and the two girls) may have lived over the shop, and so may his nephew Henry, who was indentured in 1860, and taken into partnership some time after completion of his apprenticeship seven years later.

Nothing exists to tell us whether Harris Holland's talents lay in the departments of invention, or that of business, or both. But there is a plentitude of records to confirm that his nephew was proficient in both. What we should nowadays call 'Quality Control' in manufacture was in those early days exercised by Mr Henry direct, usually in the form of polite but firm letters to the factory manager in the Harrow Road.

'This gun is not properly engraved,' he writes. 'It is going back to the shallow engraving that I so strongly objected to. I must ask you to examine the gun before it is hardened.' Later in the same letter there is an implied threat: 'Tell Crick I will not pay best price for engraving of this kind; I can get it done far better out of doors' – by which Mr Holland meant, by subcontracting the work to Birmingham. (We shall see how he treated Birmingham suppliers in a moment.) Sometimes the message from Head Office to factory is in the third person. For example on the day after the note quoted above, a letter went to the factory explaining that 'Mr Holland wishes to know why it is that the long top straps of our double rifle are now being made so flat . . . It makes them feel very awkward in the hand and there is no reason at all why they should not be rounded off more at this part. Will you kindly make a note of this in any further rifles that are made?'

Mr Holland's enquiries were not confined to quality; he also examined the accounts closely, asking 'I see March 2nd I paid £15 3s. 4d. for coke and now April 5th there is another account for coke £8 13s. 4d. Why?'

But it was quality control of the manufacture that characterises most of this correspondence. Why were defects not spotted at an earlier stage? The 'horrible colour' of the hardening of Mr Upton's gun; the improvement made to the stock when Carver's oil is used instead of ordinary oil, etc. etc. And Mr Holland, when necessary, calls upon his own experience in the factory – 'I consider it a fuss to talk about the weight of the action. When I was a workman I made a rifle for

Sir Samuel Baker weighing 22lb and there was no fuss in those days!' (The fact is that these big bore rifles were obsolete almost before they were introduced.)

It was clear from the correspondence that he could be rather outspoken if anything went badly wrong. 'It is most vexing,' he writes about one problem, adding, 'I cannot understand why it is that you cannot make guns according to instructions.' Another time he begins 'As I have so often said to you . . .' etc. etc.

It was not only the factory at Harrow Road that was subjected to this close scrutiny, but the sub-contractors at Birmingham who made up barrel and actions. For example Mr Holland, to Mr C. Bickley, Back of 12 Asylum Road, Birmingham,

'If you send us any further barrels chambered in such a manner, we must reject them. There is no difficulty in working to the standard shotgun chambers, and if you tell me that you cannot do this we shall have to make other arrangements.'

This close attention to detail was motivated by his determination to see that no gun sent out by Hollands was less than the best. He writes to the factory manager, returning some guns, to say 'there is not one of them, in my opinion, fit to go out as representing best Holland guns, and certainly would not add to our reputation if they were sent out as they are – with a man like the Maharajah of Kashmir.'

The process of manufacturing guns of best type had never succeeded in breaking away from this spirit of perfection. This was not for want of trying. The gunmakers did their best to cut the amount of hand work by using more and more sophisticated machinery down the years. Indeed, 'hand made' is in a way a misleading expression. 'Best' gun and rifle makers as a breed have always sought to de-skill these operations by use of improved machinery, and at the same time to produce a 'hand-finished' product. But inexorably the price of making the gun went up, and, because the business was so competitive, few if any of the makers ever charged enough for their guns until the 1960s.

Nevertheless their guns cost a comparatively large amount of money to buy (Colonel Hawker was even explaining the reason for this back in the early 1800s) simply because the 'London best' gun is made to measure. But unlike the made-to-measure suit, the more it is used, the more the gun likes it, so in one sense it can be said never to wear out. Guns made at the turn of the century can be in regular use nearly one hundred and fifty years later. Thousands of guns made in the 1880s and 1890s are still in use, and this is, in one sense, bad for business. Gunmakers like Holland do not know the meaning of 'planned obsolescence'. The difference between such a gem and a good mass-produced article is hard to explain. One way of putting it would be that the best machine-made guns are produced to a very high standard whereas the best hand-made guns are made to the highest standard. Telling the difference between the two will probably be subjective rather than objective.

The archive room at Holland's factory.

A tour of the Holland factory is one way of describing how

The factory at 906 Harrow Road (above as first occupied at the end of the last century) is still in use today by men who have 'exquisite skill in that mistery' – or craft.

this highest standard is achieved. Bear in mind that this factory was purpose-built for Henry Holland in the days of the gaslight, and each of the craftsmen who work there today has a window in the long narrow shop at which he plies his craft, just as his predecessors did nearly 100 years ago. In some respects times have changed. Some new machine tools have been introduced; the dress is more informal; many components formerly bought-in from a wide variety of sources are now made-in. But in general we are looking at a factory in which the manufacturing operations have not changed dramatically because the design of the gun is not radically different and hand work is still hand work.

The gun is still made of three basic components – the barrel, the action and the stock. The processes through which these basic components pass are in part simultaneous, and, in part, sequential. There is the barrel making and the actioning, both starting from a relatively crude forging. The wood stock blank and foreend, in contrast, may have been bought in some ten or twelve years before to be stored in the stockroom to ensure that it is fully seasoned.

A pair of barrels starts life as a solid three per cent nickel steel forging which is first balanced and turned on the outside and then drilled through to the correct size over a length of 31 inches. Hollands are unique in manufacturing barrels entirely within their own control from the solid – and this is a relatively new operation. Up to 1963, barrels were bought from Vickers-Armstrong, and when they decided to close down their plant, Malcolm Lyell and Geoffrey Brooks went to their factory and purchased plant to enable them to continue to produce at the Harrow Road factory. The barrel tubes are drilled, reamed, stress-relieved then ground and lapped out, making sure that wall-thickness is even. The barrel makers then take charge of the tubes, and each single tube, or pair, is identified individually for its end users. A simple paper form travels with the gun, naming the purchaser and noting calibre, length, chokes, the type of rib required, the weight and other relevant

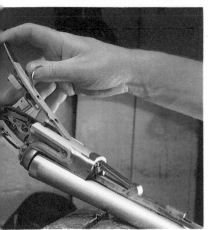

details. The barrel-makers put these tubes through a number of operations, one of the more interesting of which is the use of the old-fashioned methods of silver-brazing the tubes together, at the breech, and then soft-soldering the ribs which stiffen the barrels with pure tin (nowadays a rather expensive metal) fluxed with rosin, as this substance is non-corrosive.

All this work tends to follow conventional craft practices, but changes do take place – for example a new honing machine has been acquired to cut lapping time by two thirds.

The bores are reamed out and lapped to bring their diameter to within .004 of an inch of the finished size. Note that the outside diameters of the barrels have been steadily reduced, while the insides have been enlarged, with the object of arriving at the final correct dimensions for the finished article. The same forgings are used to make all the barrels from a .410 to a 12-bore.

The full mechanism takes the actioner about eight weeks to complete. On guns and double rifles practically every piece of it is of Holland manufacture. The action of the gun also starts as a forging, and there are numerous machining operations

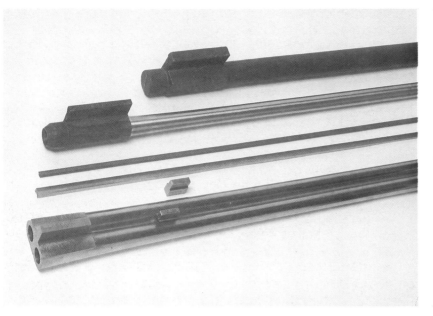

before it is given to the action shop for fitting the barrels. A spark erosion machine is a great asset in the preparation of the action, as it is capable of cutting the slots in the action to virtually finished size to receive the cocking limbs, bolt and spindle. The action shop is responsible for fitting the barrels into the action and all the mechanical working parts, i.e., ejectors, triggers, cocking parts, safety mechanism and, of course, the exterior shape of the action. It gives great pleasure to see an actioner cutting the intricate shape of the action, using a hammer and chisels.

The action shop is the foundation of the gun. If the action is poorly made, that gun will never function at its best, and no amount of rework will correct it. If it is actioned correctly, the gun will last generations. Anyone who knows guns can open and shut the gun once and instinctively know whether it had been actioned correctly or not. The 'gun' (remember that each is an idividual product, designed for a specific customer) is

Chopper lump tubes are machined from high grade British nickel steel forgings. Double rifle barrels are similarly constructed from chrome steel. Other pictures show the factory in its earliest days, and craftsmen at work today.

now at the stage where the barrel can go to the actioners' shop to have the extractors fitted into them, and the barrels jointed into the action. Each joint will be almost invisible, and it will be impossible to close the gun on a sheet of rice paper. In fact the barrels are jointed to the actions by the thickness of smoke – smoke from an oil lamp. It is during this stage that the barrels and action are sent to the London Proof House for submitting to testing. This process is described in a later chapter.

Once past the proof test, the action is finished and sent to the stocking shop for the fitting of the stock. The gun is then sent to the Shooting Grounds at Northwood where the gun regulators adjust the choke cones to give the required patterns. There are no written rules on the regulating of choke patterns – it is a matter of an experienced man knowing how to persuade a gun to throw an even pattern, and adjusting the choke by modifying the shape of the cones to obtain the result he wants. From the sportsman's point of view, this is perhaps the key phase in the manufacture of the gun, as the success of the gun in the field will depend on the art of the barrel regulator. And an art it is.

At this point, it should be confessed that it was not true to say that *every* Holland gun is manufactured to the individual requirement of a sportsman who has been fitted up at shop or school. In fact, three or four times a year, Hollands may start on the process of making components for stock. For standard 12-bore shotguns, primarily, some actions may be made up in quantity, and tubes part-processed, the aim being to have a small reserve of components to enable a gun to be put together slightly more quickly, if requested, to meet an urgent order. Normally, of course, delivery time is variable and determined by the number of guns on order at the time the order is placed. A Holland & Holland 'Royal' if pushed through all its stages with no delay will take about nine months from start to finish. Another departure from the norm is that Hollands' sporting rifles are still made on original Mauser actions which are bought-in in quantity, X-rayed and heat treated. Then modern trigger mechanisms and magazine boxes are fitted. Holland &

Holland magazine rifles have been made in this manner since the turn of the century.

To return for a moment to the Actioning Shop, there are some 20 main operations here in building the mechanism, and at Hollands it is a fact that each craftsman will be highly skilled in perhaps three or four of them, although he will know all 20 in some detail. This is because each and every man at the bench has come through the Holland apprenticeship scheme which involves a full year of off-the-bench training in the Apprentice Department, under the critical eye of the Chief Instructor, followed by four years at a chosen specialisation. Hollands take on five apprentices a year on average. In the Actioning Shop, the key skill lies in metal-to-metal fitting, for with the barrels correctly joined to the action, that soundness of joint will ensure an extended life of the gun in service. These joins cannot be seen by the naked eye, and it should be impossible to close the gun on a hair.

Another key operation of actioning, which it is difficult to describe simply in words, is the extent to which the craftsman adjusts the mechanism to take account of the profile of the individual gun. It would not do to build a standard mechanism; each gun, which is designed to suit the client perfectly, will have to incorporate cast-off or cast-on and variation of bend; the talent of the craftsman lies for example in adjusting the set strap mechanism to take account of this individual fit. One could say that this talent is an aesthetic one – the end result is a gun which is entirely fit for purpose, and, in that sense, beautiful. This is something which the standard, machine-made gun can rarely, if ever, be.

Drop forgings of low carbon steel are milled, reamed and spark-eroded to produce that basic action machinings. Specialist actioners then carefully shape and adapt the mechanism to produce the detailed variations essential to impart the stock and action with a continuous smooth line consistent with the customer's stock measurements. The simple and effective rebounding sidelock epitomises the basic concept of the 'Royal' gun.

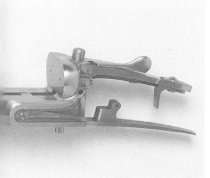

Watching a craftsman working – slow, painstaking, thoughtful – one is at once struck by his wide range of tools, many of which are of classic simplicity, and incidentally, difficult to obtain today. Indeed one of the tasks of the apprentice in his first year is to make up sets of tools to the very high specifications required. Like the young men who study Japanese pottery, and do nothing more than watch the master at work at the wheel over their first year, the Holland apprentices are not allowed to make any part for a gun during their first 12 months. Later, as has been said, the apprentice will go to work in the specialised area of his choice and aptitude, each of them under the tuition of a highly expert, full-time member of Holland's staff.

A visitor to Holland's factory will find throughout his tour not only new guns and rifles at various stages, but also guns brought in by customers for repair and replacement parts. Suppose you have a pair of guns and the barrels of one need replacement. Then Hollands must be able to make them up so that there is no detectable difference when the pair are once again a pair. Or if a stock has to be replaced, then the figure of the other gun must be matched as best it can, as well as the colour. It was said at the beginning of this chapter that a 'best' gun gets the better for use, and this is true in the sense that such a gun will not wear out. Why then should it need repair? The answer is that suppose a small amount of damage is done to the barrel by knocking it against a tree or fence – then it must be repaired and such repairs, say six times over sixty years of use, will in themselves thin down the barrels. It is repeated repairs that cause a pre-1914 'best' gun to come back to Hollands for renewal, not repeated use. This factory has by far the biggest repair shop for British sporting guns anywhere in the world, handling well over 1000 guns a year.

To continue with our tour of the Holland factory, we now go to one of the upper floors which is stocked with materials brought in from France, from Iran or from Turkey. These are the precious walnut blanks, now so scarce that special buying forays take place as soon as news arrives that a new source of

Once the grain has been filled, repeated polishing at the factory imparts a finish which should last for a lifetime, if an occasional touch of linseed oil is administered by the owner.

the treasured wood has been found. Walnut of the right kind was always traditionally available from France until, in World War I, a major proportion of the indigenous trees was felled to find stocks for infantry rifles by the hundred thousand. What a loss this was, to those who valued the walnut for the stock of a 'best' gun.

It is not as if any old part of the walnut tree will meet the gunmaker's requirements. All the wood comes from the tree at about ground level because he wants the straight grain of the trunk for the head and hand and the beautiful figuring of

Walnut stock blanks in the factory may take three or four years to mature.

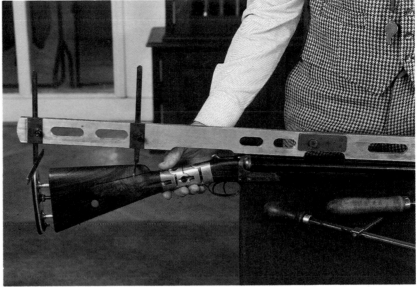

ABOVE RIGHT: *A bend jig being used to measure the adjustable try-gun to obtain a customer's exact stock requirements.*

the root for the stock (which may be gnarled and twisted, and would therefore be useless for the slimmer handling part of the gun). Walnut is strong but not, relative to other woods, heavy. The blank itself may be heavy, but a length for a rifle or a shorter stock for a shortgun will be quite light to handle – the latter weighing perhaps one pound when finished. Equally important to those who relish the look of the gun, few woods can match walnut for figuring or for grain.

The wood for a bolt action rifle can be pre-machined to an approximate size but the stock of a shotgun must be cut to the fit of the individual user to make it easy for him to handle in the more complex task of 'snap-shooting' at his target. So a customer will, like as not, visit Holland's store of blanks to select the wood of his choice, taking account of his particular views on colour, figuring and so on. At least one in three of Holland's customers today make such a personal selection, and the proportion is increasing.

It may take three to four years for the moisture content of the wood to be right (this is checked by weight and electronically), before the blank goes into the stocking shop for cutting to size. When rough stocked, what is called the 'white' gun has, as explained, been to the Proof House and to the Shooting Ground for regulation. On return the wood is finished off, oiled and chequered. On a bolt-action rifle an ebony tip may sometimes be fitted. The barrels, after they have been highly polished will also be blacked by the traditional rusting process – this is virtually the last operation of finishing.

Our final visit is to the small engraving shop where exquisite work is produced by Holland's own craftsmen – perhaps a conventional floral design, or a lion leaping from the undergrowth; St Mark's Square in Venice or family portraits; miniatures of great historic battles, or partridge, pheasant or feathered fowl. But more of this later, more of the gold embellishments, the functional screws turned into things of beauty. All in all, some 750 hours of craftsmen's time will have gone into the making of each gun or rifle. The original order received from the showroom is examined to see if all the client's instructions and specifications have been followed in

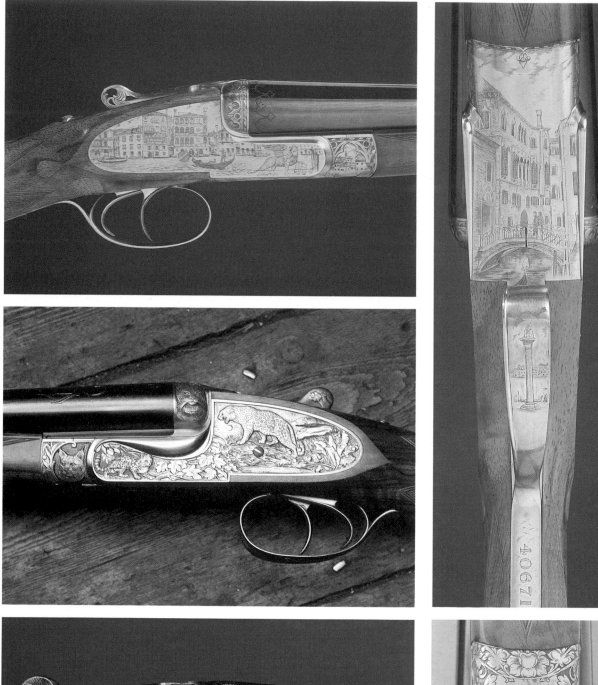

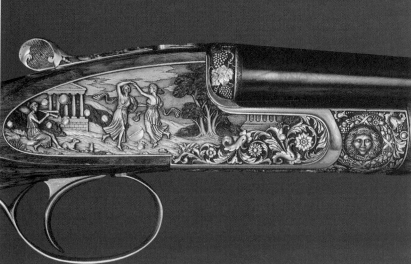

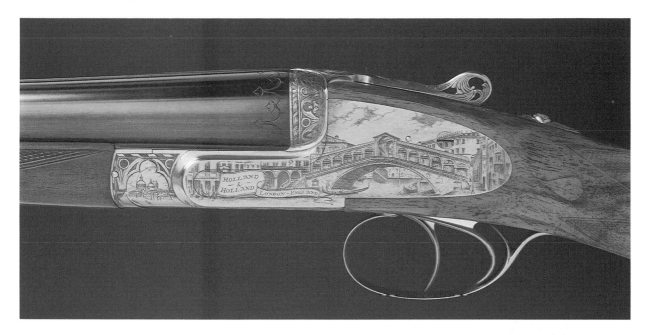

In the small engraving shop at the factory, exquisite work is produced by the craftsmen.

every detail, which will include checking if the trigger pulls to the correct weight; if the balance of the gun, the stock measurements, and the overall weight of the gun are correct; if the safety catch flies back to safe immediately when the top lever is pushed to the open position; if the chambers and bores or barrels are polished to mirror finish; and if the blows of the tumblers are heavy enough to hit the strikers so that they detonate the cartridge. Then the outward appearance of the gun is checked: is the grain of the wood completely filled in; are there any wood diamonds in the chequering to the stock fore-end and butt missing or chipped; is the gun too tight to open (a complaint from some customers who do not realize that a new gun is like a new automobile engine, it needs 500 cartridges to ease it in just as a car requires running in)?

When all the tests and examinations have been carried out, the gun is sent to the showroom, where it is again carefully examined by the senior sales staff. This will not be a mechanical inspection, as the salesman is viewing the gun from a different point of view from that of a factory craftsman. He will know his client's likes, dislikes and personality. He must judge the gun from his client's point of view and be satisfied that on handing over the best London gun, the client will realize that his patience and his money have rewarded him with one of the finest hand-built products this country can produce.

In an earlier chapter it was explained how the company had expanded its capital base in order to provide more modern facilities for gunmaking. By 1990, with the backing of Chanel, the Company business plan included a major redevelopment of the Harrow Road factory. To be completed by 1991, this would not only update the facilities for the manufacturing staff in London, and for the gun and rifle design and development programme, but would also incorporate improved ware-housing for long-term storage of customers' weapons.

This programme would give the potential to increase output of Royal guns and rifles (to which a new Royal over-and-under gun was being introduced) with the intention of returning to

The 20-bore prototype of the new 'Royal' over-and-under gun, completed in July 1990.

traditional pre-war delivery times well below the current 2-3 years. To help achieve this, the Tame Road factory, which had previously concentrated on Cavalier and Northwood boxlock production, was to be used in the interim for production of raw componentry for the Harrow Road factory and the repair and refurbishment of second-hand guns for Bruton Street. Tame Road would continue in its other role as supplier of barrels, actions and components to the British gun trade. The company's design and development department, which had been set up during the previous two years, was destined to be based in London once the facilities at Harrow Road had been redeveloped.

The company had already taken the decision to re-enter production of over-and-under guns which had ceased in the mid 60's. Two models had been considered and by June 1990 the first, a prototype Royal sidelock, had been completed in 20-bore. This gun is a radically redesigned version of the earlier model retaining only the bolt in original form. In respect of cocking, ejection and striking, significant improvements had been made in mechanical efficiency and hence reliability. Outwardly, the gun is sleek with a shallow action body which gives handling characteristics usually only associated with side-by-side guns.

It was originally expected that four prototypes would be necessary to prepare for commercial production. However, progress with the first gun was so good that it was expected that design would be completed in a second prototype. Work on the first customer orders and a twelve bore prototype would therefore begin in 1991.

The increasing interest in Europe, and especially the United States, in 'sporting' clay pigeon shooting gave rise to the second gun of a type neither Holland & Holland nor any other

The first .700 rifle.

British maker had previously developed. (The typical clay pigeon over/under had hitherto been the unchallenged product of America and Continental Europe.)

The prototype model 12-bore will have trunnion-jointed barrels and screw-in choke tubes. The action has trigger-plate lockwork (similar in principle to that of the Dickson Round-Action) which will be detachable and have a fully selective single trigger. The stock is secured by a stockbolt but, due to an innovative method of attachment, it allows a wide variety of stock fitting not usually possible in clay pigeon guns.

In January 1989, Holland & Holland introduced the .700 H&H nitro express. This was their first new calibre since the .244 H&H magnum of 1955 and it was the culmination of a project started in 1986 when Mr. William J. Feldstein Jr. of California had asked for a 600-bore. The request was refused in deference to the owner of "The last .600" (see page 143), whereupon Mr. Felstein suggested a .700 instead!

This had never been done, and so a development project was set up involving Holland & Holland and Brass Extrusion Laboratories, then of Bensenville Illinois, and Jeff McDonald of Woodley Bullets, Australia. Following the demise of the British metallic cartridge industry, Brass Extrusion had developed a fine reputation from their revival of the old English big game calibres and their experience was to be essential during the cartridge design and pressure testing phase of 1987 and 1988. The "First .700" Royal sidelock double rifle was thus completed in November 1989 and with its 26″ barrels chambered for a 3½″ case the 1000 grain bullet delivers an awesome 9050 ft. lb muzzle energy at 2000 ft per second. It was exhibited at the Safari Club International Convention in Reno, Nevada, in January 1990 and successfully hunted in Africa in February 1990.

7

The Oldest Form of
Consumer Protection

The Proof House

In a small room in the back of a Georgian building near the boundary of the City of London a man carefully pours into a cartridge case 60–80% more than the amount of powder used in a standard cartridge. He then fills it with the prescribed amount of shot. Next he takes a pair of barrels, an action stripped to its basic parts, the firing pin and locking mechanism, and places them in a carriage apparatus. After closing the door of the room, he pulls a remote control toggle which fires the gun. A nearby storeroom contains examples of every size and type of cartridge. Each one of these had been made up by the man or his assistant, and carefully checked to ensure that it packs up to five tons of pressure.

The man is the Proof Master of the London Proof House, of the Worshipful Company of Gunmakers of the City of London, Mr Alfred Bedford. As every gunmaker and most sportsmen will know, it is illegal to sell a gun, or to import one for sale, that has not passed under the expert attentions of Mr Bedford, a man of remarkable experience, who last year cast his eye down 25,000 or more barrels at his Proof House, the oldest in Europe.

To be specific, proof is the compulsory and statutory testing of every new shotgun or other small arm before sale to ensure, so far as is practicable, its safety in the hands of the user. Reproof is the similar testing of a small arm which has previously been proved. Both necessarily involve the firing through the barrel of a considerably heavier load than is customary in the shooting field, thereby setting up pressure and stress on barrel and action much in excess of the pressure generated by standard load cartridges. Such pressure should, and is intended to, disclose weakness in guns, whether new or used, for it is preferable that weakness be found at a Proof House rather than in the field where personal injury may result.

Proof in Great Britain dates back to 1637, when the Gunmakers' Company of London was granted its Royal Charter. Proof was necessary to protect the public against the many unsound arms then being made and sold, which not only endangered the public but indirectly brought discredit upon reputable gunmakers. The Gunmakers' Company secured its Ordinances in 1670 and from that time was enabled to enforce Proof in and around London. The original proof marks are still in use today.

A record of the past at the Proof House, London.

The Proof House in Commercial Road, near the Tower of London.

The Birmingham Proof House was established in 1813 by Act of Parliament requested and obtained by the Birmingham gun trade at its own expense. At a considerably earlier date private Proof Houses were in use in Birmingham. Marks similar to those used at one of them, controlled by the gunmaker Ketland, became the first proof marks of the officially established Birmingham Proof House. So since 1813 it has been an offence to sell or offer for sale an unproved arm anywhere in the United Kingdom.

The present law on the subject is to be found in the Gun Barrel Proof Acts 1868, 1950 and 1978 and various Rules of Proof, but particularly those of 1925, 1954 and 1984. The maximum prices per barrel which may be charged for proof are also set down in the Gun Barrel Proof Act of 1950 and subsequent statutory orders.

The Proof Acts lay down that no small arm may be sold, exchanged or exported, exposed or kept for sale or exchange or pawned unless and until it has been fully proved and duly marked. The maximum penalty is £1000 for each offence, but with provision for higher penalties where, for instance, the sale of a number of guns constitutes one offence. Alteration to or the forging of proof marks is a more serious offence.

Arms previously proved and bearing apparently valid proof marks are deemed unproved if the barrels have been enlarged in the bore beyond certain defined limits or if the barrel or action has been materially weakened in other respect. The offence in dealing in unproved arms is committed by the seller, not by an unwitting purchaser.

The importation of unproved arms into the United Kingdom

The Proof Master examines a barrel before proofing . . . and an imported weapon . . . he fires it . . . and applies the proof mark.

is also subject to control. Notification of importation has to be given to both Proof Houses within seven days and/or the arms have to be submitted to proof within twenty-eight days of arrival in this country. These regulations do not apply to small arms imported by any person for his own personal use while they remain his own property. Penalties for offences are similar to those for the sale of unproved arms. Until 1980, there was reciprocal agreement for recognition of certain foreign proof marks by international agreement, and since that date the United Kingdom has been a member of the International Proof Commission (the C. I. P.). *Rules, Regulations and Scales of Proof,* a schedule to the Proof Act, are the working instructions of the two Proof Houses. The rules specify the loads to be used in proof, standards of view and the marks to be impressed on guns which pass proof, together with much detail as to bore and chamber dimensions, the specifications of proof powders and service pressures. New Rules of Proof are drawn up from time to time by Proof Committees of the Worshipful Company of Gunmakers and of Birmingham. The latest Rules of Proof are those of 1984, but proof under earlier Rules of 1875, 1887, 1896,

RIGHT: *Makers' proof marks c1660–1780 and a few proof marks applied at a later date.*

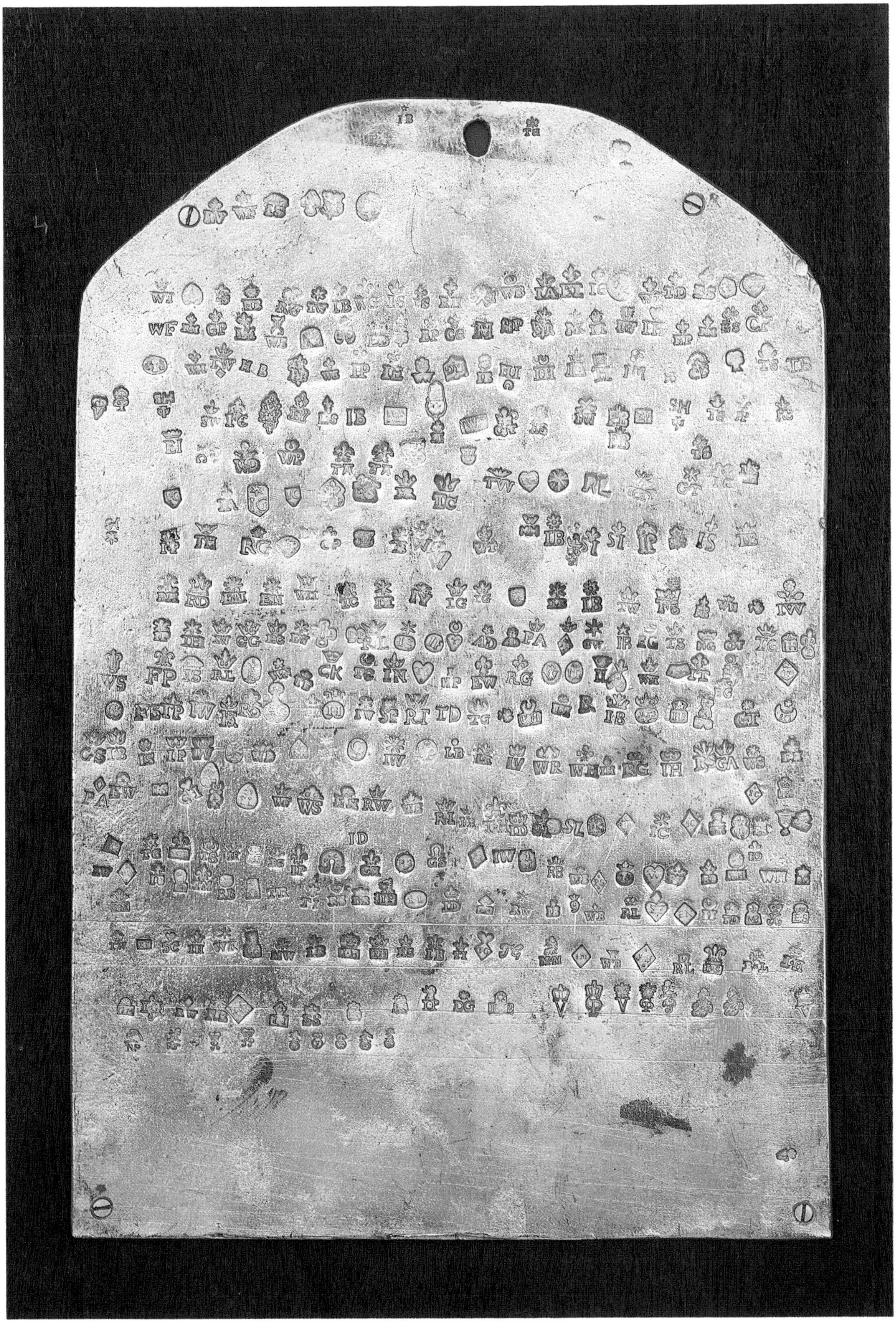

1904, 1916 and 1925 remains valid provided that the barrel or action has not been materially weakened or altered so that it no longer conforms with the proof marks. Mr Henry Holland was instrumental in drawing up the Rules of Proof in 1896 and 1904. Seventy years later, the retiring chairman of the Proof House committee, Mr Lawrence of Purdeys, came to Holland & Holland to ask that he be succeeded by Mr Geoffrey Brooks, production director of the firm, whom he acknowledged to be the most respected gunmaker in England. Mr Brooks did take on the task, and was responsible for drawing up new Rules in the early 1980s.

Many shotguns proved under Proof Rules before 1904, when the nitro proof marks were introduced, and some shotguns proved before 1925, when nitro proof became compulsory, were proved only for use with Black Powder. Such guns will not bear any of the nitro proof marks. Whilst guns proved for Black Powder may be but are unlikely to be legally proved, they must be deemed unsuitable for use with present-day cartridges unless and until they pass nitro proof.

Reproof, or the further test of a gun after its original proof, may be necessary for a variety of reasons. If mishandled or neglected a gun may be damaged or weakened, even in a short period of service, so that work necessary to return it to serviceable condition may render invalid the proof marks upon it. Indications of weakness may only be apparent to those trained to recognise them.

Any individual may submit arms for proof or reproof direct to either of the Proof Houses, but it is more usual and generally more satisfactory for all concerned that arms be submitted through a gunmaker, who has probably inspected the gun at regular intervals.

Primarily this is because the majority of old guns require attention prior to proof. Proof regulations require that shotgun barrels shall be 'struck-up' and smooth and that the insides shall be clean. Pitting should be removed so far as is practicable, bulges knocked down and dents raised. Actions should be in good safe working order and tight on the face to resist the increased strain of proof pressure. Since stocks, and

Mr Henry Holland (No 1) at the Gunmakers' Association in 1929.

The crest of the Worshipful Company of Gunmakers.

particularly those with unusual 'bend' or 'cast', are not designed to withstand the heavy recoil of proof, it is customary for the wood to be removed. Indeed, the Proof Houses do not accept responsibility for damage to stocks resulting from proof. So to fulfil these requirements the preparation necessary will best be undertaken by a gunmaker who is accustomed to submitting to proof.

To return to the London Proof House in Commercial Road, London, the remarkable thing is that so many guns are subject to the proof tests each year. The process of proofing is, as has been described: the firing, under laboratory conditions, of the barrels to ensure that their condition is satisfactory. After the test, the Proof Master Mr Bedford will examine the barrels again, to see what differences if any there are between the barrel or barrels after firing and what he has noted before. He clearly knows exactly what he is looking for, but remarks Mr Bedford, 'In time, one has a feeling for guns.' Another remarkable thing about his House is the variety of guns on the premises. A ten-foot long punt gun from Norfolk, a cannon which the owner is anxious to fire for fun on ceremonial occasions, box after box of brand new automatic weapons, and finally every conceivable size and shape of shotgun, rifle, pistol, of every period and from every country of manufacture.

How is the size of the load appropriate for proofing a particular gun calculated? Mr Bedford will make up his cartridges to the appropriate power and then, to ensure that they produce that power when tested, submit a sample batch from his production to a pressure test.

Guns do, of course, regularly fail the proof test, whether they are barrels undergoing a provisional proofing for the manufacturer, or older guns being checked for serviceability. In the event of a reject, the gun may, at the owner's expense, be repaired and resubmitted. If they fail again and again, and the submitter accepts that further attempts at repair are unlikely to succeed, the existing proof marks upon the barrels and/or action will be defaced or barred out, and it is of course unlawful for a weapon to be sold with defaced proof marks unless later proof marks have been impressed.

'Thanks to Mr Holland for all His Trouble'

The School

'We have, perhaps, a pleasant fellow, one only too anxious to do credit to his gun if he knew how, but who is ignored by his sporting acquaintances when they select their shooting guests, for they individually say, "There's Charlie Wing-Em, slaving away at his work in London, the best chap in the world. I would give anything to ask him to join our shooting party, for we are all devoted to him; but what *can* I do? – he seldom hits a bird, and, if he does, it goes away wounded. We must invite him down instead to our church bazaar in the summer".' So wrote Payne-Gallwey. Things have not changed.

Indeed, much worse things than this are said today about the 'Ready, Shoot, Aim' school, as they are sometimes called in the United States. It would not do for a book concerned with gunmakers to imply that it is possible to shoot badly with one of their guns, but anecdotes about bad shots will be found in many shooting books, notably in the chapter 'Shooters' in the *Badminton* book *Shooting,* written by Lord Walsingham and Sir Ralph Payne-Gallwey Bt. in 1889.

Sir Ralph, one of the greatest guns of his day, and, as we shall see, a keen punt-gunner, wrote also for the *Badminton* magazine, from which we take this description of a visit he paid to Holland's school at Kensal Green in the summer of 1896.

'I will endeavour to describe,' he says modestly, 'a visit I lately paid to Messrs. Holland's "shooting school". Let me state (the public is *so* suspicious nowadays) that I have *no* shares in the affair. Nor, indeed, could I have, as it is the private property of the New Bond Street firm. I write thus because it is, I believe, the proper form of preface to any favourable notice of those folk who supply one's wants, whether guns or wine.

'First of all you jump into a hansom cab, let us imagine in Pall Mall, and in twenty minutes, or in about one cigarette and a half, there you are at the shooting school, ensconced in a comfortable arm-chair in the verandah of a luxurious pavilion situated in rural, well-timbered grounds. You may also journey, if you prefer it, to Kensal Rise Station, and in this way escape the dangers of a hansom; but come somehow, and you will learn to shoot if, that is, you cannot do so already. I will suppose you have arrived. Mr Henry

Holland, or perhaps his clever partner Mr Froome (the best shot of the day with a sporting rifle, and the best regulator of one besides), if the latter is not busy plating an "Express" for the Highlands, or a "Paradox" for India or Africa, hands you for inspection, and explains the mechanism of, some of the bright new guns that stand racked in a row hard by. You would like to be a Rothschild for the moment and buy them all, or, let us say, *only* half a dozen, and you feel (in the security of a lounge chair, and the period summer) you could play the very deuce with them on the tallest pheasants and the fastest driven grouse ever seen.

As you smoke your cigarette, chat on guns and game, and hear from Mr Holland (a keen and practical game-shooter and preserver himself) of his good bags of partridges in Cambridgeshire during the past season, you are rather inclined to view with disdain the efforts of the two or three gentlemen who occasionally miss the clay pigeons that are being thrown up (from below the level of the ground) in front of the pavilion.

Wait a bit, for you will presently find that double rising clay pigeons (and single ones too – pray forgive so

Today's high tower (100ft) is rather more elegant than its predecessor.

The pavilion in the old days 'contained every convenience for visitors, including a motor garage'. Today it has a car park and a helicopter pad.

impertinent a suggestion) are not so easy to turn into dust at thirty to forty yards as you fancy, especially with a good breeze behind them.

We will now, gun in hand, inspect the various targets and the different appliances for transforming a shooter – such as the rather dubious friend who is with us – from a bad marksman into a good one.

The first test is No. 1.

Here we observe the images of six black pigeons vividly portrayed against the surface of an immense white-washed iron target. These pigeons appear at intervals of a few seconds, one by one here and there over a large space, and then, after a moment's exposure, vanish. The shooter as he stands opposite the target sees nothing but a great blank wall. He is, however, directed to throw up his gun in a natural manner and fire at each pigeon, as it appears for an instant, on the front of the target. The shooter has to fire quickly, too, for he has no leisure allowed him by the pigeon to dwell on his aim, a fatal habit when the gun is used on game. When all six pigeons have been independently shot at, one bird only being seen at a time, they are then uncovered collectively, and for the present, thus they are permitted to remain.

The shooter's gun, with which he has been performing so poorly, is now taken gently but firmly out of his hands (resistance is useless in the presence of three or four anxious and stalwart attendants) and the uncanny looking try-gun is substituted, with which strange concern he now blazes away at the pigeons as they appear and disappear.

BELOW: *The factory management testing guns at the shooting school – date unknown.*

Our friend at first makes a sad show with the try-gun; but little by little he places the shot nearer and nearer to each pigeon till at length he plasters them, one after the other, all over on pretty nigh every occasion he pulls the trigger.

Before this end is attained, and between each shot, Mr Holland has twisted, screwed, and bent, in all ways, the stock of the try-gun, and though this part of the curious weapon is as complicated to look at as a sewing machine, or the inside of a clock, it is in reality simplicity itself. Anyhow, the stock of the try-gun is now fixed in a position that causes our friend to spread the shot from its barrel smack on a pigeon, whenever one is exposed to view, short as this exposure is.

Here is, anyhow, something gained to start with; for, do as he would, he was quite unable to shoot half so accurately with his own gun at these same pigeons. The fact is the try-gun has been gradually and carefully altered in form to suit the eye and figure of our friend, and would show a very different bend and set-off from his own gun were the two contrasted.

Our friend's spirits are rising; he is interested, he says little, but, like the sailor's parrot, he is evidently thinking a good deal. He is no doubt pondering to himself, 'By Jove, there must be a lot more in the fit of a gun than I thought; fancy my living all these years and never realising it before!'

It is, though, not the mere fact that a gun needs to fit a shooter, we all know *that*; the trick is, *how* to fit the gun to the shooter, and here is where the try-gun, adequate moving targets, and an experienced gun-fitter come in,

Even in Payne-Gallwey's day there were lady pupils.

BELOW: *Management testing once more – date still unknown.*

whether to alter a gun, or to tell in what manner a new one should be shaped to match our separate peculiarities.

Our friend has now a gun in his hand, with which he can kill straight-forward shots at birds flying from him about level with his eye, and he is also able to account for a bird rising ahead and flying rapidly skyward. His next lesson, or test of the fit of his gun as the case may be, is to kill crossing shots, which are, perhaps, the most difficult of all.

Here we have birds flying and rabbits scampering – metal though they be – across the open spaces between the three shelters in front of the long part of the target to the right. Both birds and rabbits move with *accelerated* speed (a necessity if they are to resemble the actions of game), leaving their respective shelters at a moderate pace to dart (at the moment you are *inclined* to hang on the trigger) into hiding, just as a live creature runs to ground-cover or skims out of sight over a hedge. One rabbit or bird, or two of either, can be made at will to move as slowly or rapidly as wished across the target; and, as they are arranged to run or fly in different directions, when started in couples, this affords excellent practice for crossing or for quick right and left shots.

Here again we can instantly detect if the aim is to the right or left, high or low. Provided the aim is all right, as it should

Ladies and young women form a considerable proportion of the school's customers today.

be after the previous experiments, these crossing-shots are most useful as a final test to prove that the general fit of the gun is correct and the pull of the trigger adapted to the finger and nerve of the shooter.

By this time the shooter and the try-gun are on very friendly terms, and the former is wondering if he will ever manage to shoot as well with his own gun as he does with the try-gun. But the try-gun is now discarded; it has done its work, and our friend has a new ejecting hammerless placed in his hands, the shape of the stock of which is as near as possible to the shape the stock of the try-gun has finally attained under Mr Holland's manipulation. Our next move is to the flying birds that approach the shooter for all the world like driven game. No better practice could be desired than these clay pigeons, sent overhead as they are, for testing the fit of a gun, for teaching the beginner to kill game, and, above all, for instructing him in the safe handling of his gun. They are also admirable aids to *concluding* the fit of a gun.

'Why, here is my own gun come back!' says our friend. 'Yes, and what is more, it has made a journey to the factory whilst we have been so occupied, and is now altered to the shape the try-gun assumed when it was proved to suit you, as evidenced by your success with it at the various targets.'

A rifle regulator at work on the recently reconstructed 100 yards range.

Inside the new shooting school pavilion, built in 1982.

'Take your old gun again, put a couple of dozen cartridges in your pocket, and walk through this rough grass and young covert,' requests Mr Holland, 'and see what you can kill. You must not expect pheasants and partridges, for they are not in season; but we shall, at all events, soon discover if your aiming powers have benefited by the alteration I have made to your gun, and by your first visit to a "shooting school".

As you stroll amid the knee-deep cover, up spring pigeons here and there, at thirty to forty yards forward of you – live ones this time – and to your surprise and delight down they come too, and want no retriever either, for you are knocking all life out of them by placing the *centre* of the shot charge fair on each bird almost every time you fire. You have certainly not wasted the afternoon, for you may at length feel confident your gun fits you as it should do.

'Many thanks to Mr Holland for all his trouble; a cup of tea in the cosy smoking-room of the pavilion, and we drive back to London in good time for dinner.'

So much for the old days. Like many other gunmakers, Holland's school, situated in a part of London which was ripe for building development, was probably their most valuable asset. Some firms sold their school land in hard times in order to realise enough cash to keep going. Others, like Hollands, sold up in order to move by buying or leasing land further out of London. In the process they would enlarge or improve their facilities. Hollands moved from Kensal Rise, near the factory, to North Forty Farm, Wembley in 1913. It was held on a lease for 99 years and the chairman lent the company £3000 to effect the purchase. Kensal was described as close to the West End of London, and Wembley was only 30 minutes from Bond Street. In 1923 the freehold of Wembley was bought for £10,000 and war loan stock sold off to pay for it. *The Field* described the new school as 'very favourably circumstanced'. Then, in 1933 the school moved again to the appropriately named Ducks Hill Road, an area of 100 acres yet only 17 miles from that hub of the universe, Bond Street, or 'most convenient to London' as the brochure put it. As this was a reasonable distance for the motor car, the premises were equipped with a motor garage.

Despite all this, Colonel Holland was not an enthusiast for the school, grudgingly acknowledging that, if customers insisted on going down, they should be allowed to do so. The major change came when the famous Robert Churchill's school was closed. His chief instructor, Norman Clarke, was extremely popular with a number of influential shots, and they advised Malcolm Lyell to offer him a similar position at Hollands. Clarke became a key figure for Malcolm Lyell's policy of making the Holland school not only the best in the world, but an essential element in the company's selling

Norman Clarke was especially good with children . . . and with sportsmen like Lord Rank.

posture. The new chief instructor had a remarkable personality; he was warm, humorous, intelligent and had that most important of characteristics for a teacher, the ability to give his pupils self-confidence.

While Clarke was well-known in the shooting world when he joined Hollands, in a very short time he became a famous figure. The number of those visiting the school for instruction rose rapidly. It had been on average 500 a year during the 1950s, and had once reached 1000. Under Clarke it rapidly reached 2000 and went on climbing. What is more, the School made a profit of £2500 at the end of Clarke's first year, and the company was able to take up the option to buy it from the Holland interests by June 1963 at the agreed valuation of £10,500. And Lyell was determined to take the Holland teaching philosophy around the world, and this became possible in 1966 when Abercrombie and Fitch sponsored a visit by the two men to the USA. They were there, at A & F's 'sporting goods store' at Madison Avenue and 45th Street for over two weeks and then travelled elsewhere, fitting new purchasers and giving shooting lessons at the A & F ranges in the afternoons. Later Holland-inspired schools were set up in Europe, in Sweden and in Germany, whose instructors were trained at the school.

One aspect of Clarke's character which has inspired anecdotes was his inability to suffer know-alls gladly. One of the latter told him, 'I do not want to be interfered with while I am shooting.' So Clarke took him at his word and ignored him as he stood shooting at the first few targets. Clarke's silence was so overbearing, that the know-all finally asked him, 'What do you do? How do you instruct?' Clarke took the man's gun from him and said, 'Sometimes a shot has only a left hand, so I shoot like this.' Lifting the gun with one hand he shattered the clay. 'Sometimes a shot has only a right hand.' Clarke lifted the gun with the right arm only, and shot a clay. 'Sometimes they haven't any strength in either arm,' and he shattered a clay from the hip. 'Sometimes they can only shoot with the gun upside down,' he added and shattered another clay in that curious fashion. The know-all had enough by this time and apologised.

Another anecdote that Norman Clarke told Jeremy Clowes concerned a rich shooter who failed to break his gun to see if it was loaded on picking it up. Clarke remonstrated with him. 'But it's my gun and I know it's not loaded,' said the man. Clarke gently pointed out that he could be wrong. 'No,' said the man, 'I *know*. And I will bet you a million bucks that it isn't loaded.' Clarke told him that such a bet was meaningless as he didn't have a million dollars to lose, and to the rich man a million was not all that much. 'My bet,' said Clarke, 'is that you won't put the barrels of the gun in your mouth and pull both triggers.' The rich man would not, on consideration, take up that bet, and learnt his lesson.

Clarke was not only a great teacher and a clever psychologist, but he was also able to instruct the instructor, with the result that the school went on from strength to strength after he died of a heart attack at the school at the early age of 59. Today the school regularly copes with 5000 visitors a year, plus another 1500 who come in small groups or parties of 20 to 30 people. Some of the visitors are customers, or friends

Practice at picking a bird from a covey in one of the school's grouse butts.

of customers, who come to be fitted. Others are shots who come to improve their shooting, and they may visit for an hour or so, or half a day, or they may buy a season ticket and come as often as they can, to be instructed by one of the five instructors. Some specify that they want a different instructor on each visit. One visitor throws a party each year at the school for those friends who invite him to their places to shoot, since he has no ground of his own where he can return the hospitality. Another comes on his own, week in week out, every Thursday, rain or shine, to shoot 125 clays, but apart from that he never fires another shot, never attends a live shoot. Then there are the large and prestigious companies who bring small parties of business people to spend an afternoon or an evening at the school, in the same way that other (less imaginative) companies take their friends to play golf.

For the customers, the 'uncanny-looking fit gun' is still used as it was in Payne-Gallwey's time. In other ways, the school is somewhat different from what it was in his day. For a start there are no live birds. Then there are no metal replicas. The technique is now to use the Plating Targets and the Fitting Plates to sort out any basic problems, and then to go to (say) the middle partridge range, or the High Tower to shoot at clays as Payne-Gallwey describes. Payne-Gallwey would also have been surprised to see the shop.   One of the most interesting aspects of the school is the attention paid to the young shooter, to whom special rates are offered. This is, of course, nothing new. Back in 1936 *The Field* asserted that Holland's shooting instructors 'have some small knowledge of how to handle the young, and especially the nervous young'. The writer asked, 'What better present could the generous uncle, the benificent godfather give than, say, six days at the Badminton Shooting School? The day is gone when it was given to many of us to offer a boy a few days' shooting; the day has come when we can teach him the elements of shooting in a very few days.'

Lord Lonsdale at the opening of the new school at Wembley Park, christened the 'Badminton School' by kind permission of the Duke.

FROM : FIELD-MARSHAL THE VISCOUNT MONTGOMERY OF ALAMEIN
K.G., G.C.B., D.S.O.

ISINGTON MILL
ALTON
HANTS

TEL BENTLEY 3126

24-3-68

My dear Lyell

I duly took my grandson to your shooting school on Friday. Norman Clarke was delighted with him after only one lesson; he is a superb instructor. Henry did well with the clay pigeons; indeed he killed one with his first shot, after 30 minutes instruction.

The gun is to be sent back to you for altering the stock; it is too long, and I presume Norman Clarke has told you what alteration is needed. Can you please have the alteration to the stock done quickly.

Lord Montgomery (the Field-Marshal always personally filled-in the hyphen missed from the head of his notepaper) was one of those who supported Clarke as an instructor of the young.

Some of Holland's instructors prefer these lessons to begin at about the age of twelve, when he or she is strong enough to handle something bigger than a .410. Norman Clarke, who was especially good with children, used to believe that to give the young confidence, it was important to arrange for them to hit something – anything – early on in their first lesson. Holland's say that there is no less keenness among the young now than there has ever been, despite the high cost of guns and shooting. Of course there will always be those who believe that young people are now not what they used to be. For example, the famous Lord Ripon, writing in Payne-Gallwey's three volume *Letters to Young Shooters* said that in his day 'The young men then were keener sportsmen. I remember being hardly able to sleep on the Monday night before a big shoot, and I am sure my feelings were shared by many others of my own age. Now in the youth of the present generations, I remark a growing tendency to arrive a day later than they are invited, to be called to London by a previous engagement the day before the shooting ends, and sometimes even to 'chuck' as they euphoniously express it, a visit altogether.'

Let it be noted that while Ripon refers solely to the young *men* at his shooting parties, we have taken care to speak of young *persons*, as the young lady today may well become as keen a shot, and as good as the men. Whatever the sex of their pupils Holland's instructors believe that there are no grounds for the pessimism which Ripon expressed in the following stirring words: 'Maybe,' he mused, 'a generation will spring up to whom all these things will be a closed book; but when that day comes, England will lose her most attractive and distinguished feature and one of her most cherished traditions. For the England of whom the poets have sung for many centuries will have ceased to exist.

9

'Stiff Collars at all Times'

Diversion on Clothing

The premises from which many of the London gunmakers sold their products have, from the middle of the 19th century, been located in the posher part of the capital. Oxford Street, St James's, Mayfair and Bond Street have been typical addresses. These showrooms are much more than mere shops: they have become meeting places for shooting people from all over the world, no matter whether their quarry be big game or quail, grouse or stag. The customer wishing to order a new gun or rifle will have much to discuss when he visits the gun room, and two hours or more must be set aside if he is to do the matter justice.

There is the process of determining the fit of the stock. How long a barrel does he want? What length of chamber? How much choke? What sort of grip for the stock – pistol grip or straight hand? What kind of trigger, and what weight of trigger pull? The questions are not exactly endless, but there are a good many more than this. Once the basic specification has been discussed, Hollands usually like the new customer to visit the Shooting Grounds in order that measurements can be refined to give him the stock shape with which he will shoot his best. Stock blanks can, of course, be sent to the showroom, or, if time permits, he can visit the factory and choose from the large selection of walnut blanks stored in the racks there.

For engraving, there is a book of rubbings from previous engravings available as a guide, or sometimes a customer will supply photographs of, for example, his house or dogs for the purpose.

Holland's showroon at Bruton Street is a mass of activity; it is part gunroom, part museum, part club, and part repair shop (not that the actual work it done there, but spare parts are on occasion shipped abroad for fitting). It is the receiving point for the hundreds of guns sent to Hollands for repair or restoration every year. The matter of shipping a gun around the world is not an easy one; Jeremy Clowes recalls that one American customer always marks his box 'Biological specimens only to be opened and examined under laboratory conditions' and from experience he has found this an effective deterrent to the thief.

Cartridges have to be supplied to customers – it is part of the service – but they cannot be sent through the post, and this ensures a steady stream of callers at Bruton Street. Indeed for

The Holland & Holland Cavalier has been on the cartridges and catalogues since the turn of the century.

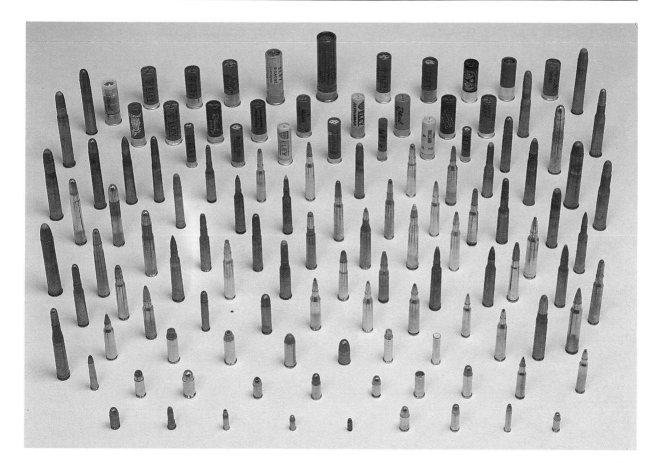

Supplying cartridges is part of the service at the shop in Bruton Street.

many a year cartridges were actually manufactured on the premises, as the following extract from the *Evening Standard*'s column written by 'The Voice of London Town' shows, just before the outbreak of the 1939 war:

Two machines like coffee grinders stand in the top windows of a shop which overlook dress shops of Bond Street. Mr Charles Fletcher, who has been at his trade for 32 years, pours coarse black powder into the maw of one of the machines and gives the handle a turn, catching some of the powder in a metal tube. He weighs the powder on a delicate balance, makes an adjustment on the machine and tries again. At last he is satisfied; the machine is issuing exactly 33 grains of gun-powder. Then he works the other machine, pouring in a bag of shot. With another balance he tests this machine's issue also, until it is giving exactly 1 oz. of shot.

Meanwhile a young assistant has been fitting 100 cartridge cases in one tray and putting 100 wads in another. Mr Fletcher shoves the first tray under his powder-machine, turns the handle ten times and there are 33 grains of powder in each, he hopes. He tests a few of them on the balance. One is one tiny grain out. Another gadget shoves the wads home. Finally, the ends of the cartridge are turned in, and there you have 100 rounds of 12-bore ammunition, all hand-made in Bond Street. "Our clients prefer hand-made to machine-made ammunition because of the greater accuracy of the charge," says a salesman.

I have walked into a gun-lined parlour of Holland & Holland Ltd., where sportsmen are fitted for their guns and their rifles. There is a customer bringing a gun to his

shoulder as though he were going to blast the front windows out. A salesman directs the fire on to himself by holding his index finger immediately under his right eye. "Sight at my finger," he says. It is not a suicide pact, just a test of sighting. The firm has "try-guns" with extending stocks to test a man's needs, and he is usually taken to the shooting grounds at Northwood before they start to make a gun for him. It supplies him with a "cross-eyed", with a bent stock, to suit a man whose left eye is stronger than his right.

A salesman shows me the "modèle de luxe," a very nice piece of shot-gun indeed with a beautifully grained stock and elaborate engraving. "Our price 150 guineas," he says. "Usually our customers order them in pairs. Of course, we have made more expensive guns than that. Some of the Indian princes used to like them inlaid with gold and precious stones. They cost about 200 guineas." "Did they provide the precious stones?" I ask. "Yes," says the salesman.

Perhaps this is the point to discourse on the vexed subject of price. After all, 40 guineas does not seem a great deal to have paid for a London 'Best' shotgun in 1887 or 125 guineas in 1939. It has already been said that most of the London

Business has broadened out from the sale of guns to other related items.

This illustration in Manton & Co's catalogue shows a Portable Machan or Shikar Ladder, a 'great boon' which was 'two coolies' load'. It was fitted with a revolving seat so that the shooter did not need to have eyes in the back of his head. Manton set up a branch in India, which published this catalogue.

5. THE STORY OF THE MAN THAT WENT OUT SHOOTING.

This is the man that shoots the hares;
This is the coat he always wears:
With game-bag, powder-horn and gun
He's going out to have some fun.

The hare sits snug in leaves and grass,
And laughs to see the green man pass.

He finds it hard, without a pair
Of spectacles, to shoot the hare.

Now, as the sun grew very hot,
And he a heavy gun had got,
He lay down underneath a tree
And went to sleep, as you may see.
And, while he slept like any top,
The little hare came, hop, hop, hop,
Took gun and spectacles, and then
On her hind legs went off again.

gunmakers sold their guns far too cheaply from the earliest days, with the result, as Colonel Hawker pointed out, that many of them ended their days in penury. Later, some saved themselves by selling off their training school land to property developers.

It was in 1965 that the Holland board took an important decision and brought up their price list by around 50 per cent, lifting the cost of a 'best' gun from £800 to £1200 at a stroke. This bold move saved them from the doldrums into which many other competitors drifted with the eventual loss of famous names like Churchill and Messrs. Atkin, Grant & Lang.

Another method of improving the commercial viability of the business was to broaden out from the sale of guns to other related items. There were respectable antecedents for doing so; after all, the famous Bishop of Bond Street (Westley Richards's agent in the early 1800s) had sold silver and jewellery as well as guns. In the 1950s and 1960s some of the London makers began timorously with clothing. Such reticence was understandable in a business which a modern marketing man would describe as totally product-orientated. True some agents, particularly overseas, had prided themselves on giving a complete range of products in their catalogues, as the illustration from a page in the India company Manton's sales literature indicates (Members of Manton's family had gone out to India to set up in business in the early 19th century). But clothing is not widely featured because it is not until comparatively recently that specially-made clothing for shooters has been *de rigeur*.

Lady Diana Cooper tells us in her memoires that her father, the 8th Duke of Rutland, had a strict rule that male guests at his house parties should wear stiff collars at all times. He did not care for the fact, she says, that this rule was relaxed when the men were out shooting. It would be one thing to wear a stiff collar in the field, but does anyone today contemplate using a

LEFT: *A young lady shooter about 1875, probably one of Holland & Holland's European customers.*

RIGHT AND BELOW: *Keeping the top hat on one's head when shooting with a muzzle-loader must have been difficult — And on horseback even more so.*

shotgun while wearing a top hat? In the earliest days, galloping across the manors after a partridge, a top hat might offer some protection to the head in the event of coming off, but walking in the fields after fur or feather, what use was a top hat? Did it not impair the vision? In any case, the hazards of shooting with a muzzle loader were formidable.

Lt.-Col. Peter Hawker, the legendary shot, wrote,

'When we look back to the copper cap, what a vast amount of trouble and anxiety the latter entailed! We many of us remember its worries: the hasty fumbling in pockets for the different wads, the caps, the powder, the shot – all neatly and systematically placed in their proper receptacle on starting the day, with apparent impossibility of confusion,

The gamekeeper, Mellors, is clearly wearing a stiff collar.

LEFT: *A German hunter equipped to shoot rabbit. Alas his gear is no longer available at the shop.*

The caption, in French, to the original picture says that the man is astonished to see a lady dressed 'en habit de chasse à pied'.

Highland Funeral, a watercolour by Lionel Edwards, showing a stalking party returning to the lodge after a successful day on the hill.

but which nevertheless, after a few shots, seemed mischeviously subject to disarrangement. One of the most original reasons for preferring breech-loaders to muzzle-loaders was once given me by the schoolboy son of a sporting farmer. 'You see sir,' quoth the youngster, 'if a gun ain't got no ramrod, your father can't lay one across your back when he isn't pleased with you out shooting.'

The danger of a muzzle-loader was no small item in the day's shoot. We often heard of first barrels exploding while second barrels were loading; of caps being jarred off; of powder flasks ignited by sparks . . . not to speak of such minor incidents as ramrods being sent flying to the clouds – or into a tree or a cow! But we have changed all that. A child could almost be taught to load a modern gun without risk.'

Before the advent of the breech-loader in the 1850s, any shooting was, according to a later author, 'a very messy business. The elegantly dressed characters in the sporting prints came home with blackened hands and faces, sooted and smelling like their guns with the oily residue of black powder. After 20 rounds or so, their guns coked up like old tobacco pipes. Their hats, after a season in the field, smelt like exploded rockets.'

He goes on to imagine the scene when the hunter returned home, quite unfit to enter the house. In the gun room (or outside the house) the weapon had to be scrubbed out with cold and then hot water from a kettle. Once this had been satisfactorily accomplished, the hunter himself had to head for the hip bath.

OVERLEAF: *Grouse shooting, an engraving dated 1878.*

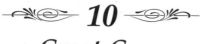

10
Great Guns

Some Edwardians at Sport – and Royalty

Those were the Old Years, the Great Days; Lady Diana Cooper tells us in her memoirs that the express trains to Scotland would be stopped especially for the Duke of Rutland's party so that they could travel easily to his estate. 'At the station we tumbled out, laden with the paraphernalia of art and sport . . . The guns, rods, cameras, easles, books and opera-scores were trotted through the village, where the children, pouring *en masse* out of school, would cheer us home'. She describes how there would be about twelve people staying for a shooting party, all with maids, valets and large dress baskets . . .

> 'The guests would arrive on Monday and my father would expect them, so that would be all right, but when they left on Friday, and a new dozen arrived, not expected by my father and generally of a much younger generation, he would greet them ashen in the face with 'What train are you taking on Monday?' It was the shock; once recovered he was happy with them all and sad to see them go. We would always be at the shooting-lunches on the moors or in fields or in the farmer's parlour, eating mutton pies, or Irish stew and jam puffs and Stilton cheese, with sips of cherry brandy or Grand Marnier to keep the cold out, while the head keeper brought in the last of the bag and was rewarded with a tumbler of neat whisky.'

The portrait of the Duke of Portland which appeared as the frontispiece to his memoirs Men, Women and Things.

A number of amusing tomes have been written about the great shots and the great shoots of the Edwardian era. Holland & Holland provided the mechanisms with which many of these eccentric men – and women – would pursue their vocation.

One of these was the 6th Duke of Portland whose shooting experiences were written up – by himself – in his volume *Men Women and Things* from which the following quotations are taken.

> 'The two best game shots I ever met were undoubtedly, in my opinion, the late Lord Ripon, formerly Lord de Grey, and Sir Harry Stonor, both wonderfully good with either gun or rifle. In discussing shooting it is never necessary to ask whether de Grey or Stonor was 'in form': for neither of them ever seems to be 'out of form'. I think Stonor, until his eyes unfortunately and sadly failed him, was the most graceful handler of a gun I ever saw, though perhaps during the

The 6th Duke of Portland, a Holland user and author of a book on stalking.

GAME KILLED BY EARL DE GREY

from 1867 to 1900

DATE	RHINOCEROS	TIGER	BUFFALO	SAMBUR	PIG	DEER	RED DEER	GROUSE	PARTRIDGES	PHEASANTS	WOOD COCK	SNIPE	WILD DUCK	BLACK GAME	CAPERCALZIE	HARES	RABBITS	VARIOUS	TOTAL
1867							8	265	1,179	741	20	22	10			719	934	115	4,013
1868							35	201	1,418	1,601	28	67	23			690	543	113	4,719
1869							35	135	1,659	1,431	26	133	37			547	443	122	4,568
1870							21	498	2,309	2,417	36	53	30			833	626	137	6,660
1871							55	1,408	1,598	1,889	50	244	42			1,093	341	225	6,945
1872							38	1,498	2,083	2,835	27	60	31			1,108	756	235	8,671
1873							25	248	2,417	3,050	95	263	85			1,027	450	591	8,251
1874						3	5	90	2,878	2,345	229	462	131	5	4	1,200	302	1,200	8,854
1875							3	287	2,882	3,225	176	461	208			1,376	576	743	9,937
1876							3	1,554	3,394	4,110	30	25	37			1,248	890	266	11,557
1877						2	4	2,032	2,359	4,235	35	45	33	11	11	1,496	1,044	309	11,616
1878						4	9	1,669	3,378	4,679	43	44	55	5	6	2,152	667	503	13,214
1879							4	1,344	630	3,140	132	92	62	9	11	1,125	287	215	7,051
1880		9	6	18	31	73	12	1,131	682	531	9	47	54	26	5	501	141	408	3,684
1881							5	1,566	3,465	5,014	26	14	43			1,058	791	166	12,154
1882	2	2	6	1	66	104	10	3,025	2,123	2,370	14	21	44			464	1,122	117	9,491
1883							5	2,896	1,845	6,119	157	84	155			918	1,386	319	13,884
1884							10	3,073	3,523	4,347	134	70	70			713	1,896	453	14,289
1885							5	2,015	2,788	4,620	104	23	31			589	2,547	108	12,830
1886							20	1,989	1,463	3,383	105	87	72			357	786	349	8,611
1887							57	2,258	3,785	3,387	104	3	12			415	2,328	237	12,586
1888							4	3,060	853	5,072	31	151	10			307	1,523	85	11,096
1889							5	3,081	5,751	6,182	100	109	14	38	8	1,747	1,069	135	18,239
1890								2,006	7,002	6,498	172	105	28			1,446	1,120	123	18,500
1891								2,277	1,699	5,794	34	13				711	406	271	11,205
1892							1	1,412	6,784	5,580	7	10	5			453	1,233	281	15,766
1893								2,441	8,732	5,760	66	7	42			837	914	166	19,135
1894								2,295	7,563	5,034	76	7	12			935	580	222	16,695
1895							1	1,272	3,561	6,101	11	13	17			352	1,040	210	12,478
1896								2,042	2,613	8,514	13	11	4			314	557	177	14,852
1897							1	2,237	1,904	7,850	67	10	47			358	828	152	14,024
1898								1,693	1,200	3,432	18	3	6			169	298	144	6,963
1899								870	1,209	4,605	19	2	57			205	609	137	7,763
1900								1,033	1,322	6,762	24	8	95			223	819	141	10,427
	2	11	12	19	97	186	382	56,460	97,759	142,363	2,218	2,769	1,612	94	45	27,686	29,858	9,175	370,728

A summary of Lord Ripon's remarkable game book.

Lord Rothschild, whose family were Holland customers.

Prince F. Dhuleep Singh (right) shot with three guns and two loaders. He learned to shoot at the estate of the Rothschilds.

day's shooting he did not kill quite so much as did de Grey. I think de Grey killed about twenty-five birds to Stonor's twenty; but for all that, I do not believe that Stonor missed more shots than de Grey, if as many.

'I remember four extremely high birds passing over de Grey on the Groveley Beat at Wilton where the birds fly exceptionally high. He killed the first three quite dead, and I said to myself, 'The fourth has escaped.' But no! – it came down quite as dead as the others. One remarkable thing about de Grey's shooting was that one hardly ever saw a bird even flutter after he had fired at it.

I knew him exceedingly well, for in 1882 I went to India with him when his father was Viceroy and we shot together in Nepal. He was very often my guest at Welbeck for partridge and pheasant shooting. His game book is an extraordinary record; the rhinoceros mentioned at the head of the list must be those I saw him kill dead, right and left with a four-bore rifle, from the back of an elephant in Nepal.

'De Grey, I believe, was always accurate when asked the amount of game he had killed, and he did not exaggerate. I remember quite well that after a partridge drive my agent,

Mr T. Warner Turner, asked him how many birds he had killed. He counted the empty cartridge cases, of which there were 14 and said, "I have killed thirteen birds." Mr Turner told the keeper, whose duty it was to pick up the dead game to report to him the number of birds he found where de Grey had been shooting, and when he had done so, he told Mr Turner that there were 13.'*

The Duke tells an excellent story about a novice sportsman. He writes:

'A keeper who had been accustomed to load for de Grey was employed to load for a novice sportsman. When the novice had missed far more birds, during a drive, than he had killed, he asked the loader, "Say, how many would Lord de Grey have killed?" "Three times as many as you did." At the next drive he fired two barrels into the brown of a pack, and down came four birds. He turned in triumph to the same loader and remarked, "I guess that beats your Lord de Grey. How many would *he* have killed with that shot?"'*

'When I was travelling with de Grey in India, he advised me always to be very careful about what he called my "foot-work" when shooting; and he said he considered correct footwork to be of the greatest importance, though it was only too often neglected. (Norman Clarke always said the same – plus correct gun-mounting.) He said that in order to shoot well, it was absolutely necessary to bring the right leg well round in firing at birds passing to one's left, and vice-versa; and that, in firing at birds passing straight over one's head, the feet should be in line, and well apart. He added – and I entirely agree – that, if one did not do this, one was

Lord Lonsdale deer-shooting in Lowther Park, near Kendal in the Lake District.

Edward VII, when Prince of Wales, gave up fox hunting, and shooting became his passion. But according to Lord Ripon, the greatest shot of the day, he was not always on form.

*A parallel story is that of Sir John Willoughby who dared to contend de Grey's account of the number of cartridges used to kill an astonishing number of birds. He was subsequently proved wrong.

The Duke of Westminster's shooting party at The Tower, Llanarmon, Wales.

Edward's son, George V, was however said to be one of the four best shots in the country. He is seen here at Balmoral.

very apt to fire behind birds, and either to miss them or to hit them in the tail.

'De Grey used hammer guns and black powder long after everyone else had given them up. He had his guns handed to him at full-cock, which possibly accounted for the extreme rapidity with which he shot.

'I several times asked de Grey whom he considered the best shot he had ever seen, and each time, without hesitation whatever, he replied, "Walsingham, with regard to both rapidity and accuracy." (Thomas, sixth Lord Walsingham, born 1843, died 1919.) It is rather curious that Lord Walsingham was the Hon. T. de Grey before he succeeded; so the best two shots in England at that time were Lord de Grey and Tommy de Grey. Of course they were often confused.

'Tom de Grey was a remarkable, a brilliant, and an eccentric person. He was a first-class scientist, one of the best entomologists in the world of his day, rich when he inherited and bankrupt when he died. His fortune went partly in the lavish manner in which he ran everything connected with sport or science, but in the main it was caused when Walsingham House, which stood where the Ritz now stands, was pulled down and London's first block of flats was built on its site. They were badly designed, proved a failure, and, if I remember right, Walsingham lost the better part of a quarter of a million pounds over it.'

The Duke of Portland's head keeper, Donald Ross, introduced heather burning in 1859 long before it was generally realised that this regenerated a plentiful supply of heather for the young grouse stock. By 1871 the total on his moors had

reached 2230 brace and the numbers kept going up. This success with grouse was later matched by his record partridge bags:

'In 1894 and 1895 partridge driving was first practised at Welbeck and Clipstone. In 1896 partridge driving really commenced. The peak year was 1929, when 3,349 brace were killed. In 1927 practically no partridges were shot at all, and in 1928 only 847 brace were killed. 1934–35 was also an excellent season, when 3,268 brace of partridges were killed, and in addition, 5,148 pheasants, all wild birds, as none had been hand-reared for several years. I believe more partridges have been killed in recent years at Welbeck than at any other place in England. On one occasion no less that 270 brace, and several times well over 200 brace, have been killed there in four drives.'

The Duchess of Bedford, one of the early women shots, complained about the length of her skirts.

PARTRIDGE BAGS AT WELBECK

1879	5	1894	768	1909	1,487	1924	4,338
1880	40	1895	1,317	1910	1,805	1925	3,937
1881	319	1896	2,948	1911	4,140	1926	2,576
1882	418	1897	2,351	1912	238	1927	6
1883	428	1898	3,494	1913	726	1928	1,095
1884	961	1899	3,406	1914	4,868	1929	6,698
1885	961	1900	4,155	1915	2,718	1930	3,426
1886	601	1901	5,504	1916	1,057	1931	793
1887	2,119	1902	4,008	1917	1,964	1932	582
1888	1,194	1903	4,128	1918	2,573	1933	3,203
1889	1,920	1904	4,160	1919	3,235	1934	6,537
1890	1,688	1905	4,380	1920	126	1935	5,245
1891	961	1906	6,183	1921	3,952	1936	1,270
1892	770	1907	220	1922	2,208		
1893	1,184	1908	1,339	1923	3,102		

As a postscript, one might add that the Duke said, 'When I look back at the game book, I am quite ashamed of the enormous number of birds that we sometimes killed. This is a form of shooting which I have no desire to repeat.'

In his article 'Some Great Shoots and Great Shots' Wentworth Day made an attempt to discover who were the best twelve shots in the United Kingdom at that time. He sent out 500 letters to representative landowners, shooting men, head keepers and others. The 'winner' was another Holland customer, Captain Ivan Cobbold of Glenham Hall. But Wentworth Day concludes his tally with these words:

'But the mere mechanics of markmanship are no criterion of the sport or of the true enjoyment of shooting. It is not the bag which matters – a true word as true as when it was first spoken. Shooting to the man who really loves it is as a picture-book of memories, cameos of recaptured dreams.
'Bitter dawns on the tide-line; moonlit nights and the mystery of a marsh moved by a quiet wind like mice in the reeds; the high blue of a Norfolk sky on a November morning outside one of those deep, warm fir coverts which hold pheasants and golden partridge, wrens, woodcocks

Holland and Holland gun and rifle case labels show the extensive use made of royal warrants over the years. Top left is one of the earliest surviving Holland labels.

and clattering clouds of wood-pigeons; snipe on an Irish bog seen against the far vision of a Kerry lake; grouse speeding at your head, coming above bee-murmurous heather, hot in the August sun; partridges springing like brown bombshells from the green ocean of a field of mangold-wurzels. These are memories which remain, pictures painted on the mind.

'Those are the visions of the shooting man, the heritage of his happy experience. The whisper of wind in wet woods, the strong sea smell of tide-bared muds, the silence of a Highland glen in hot September, the whisper of the wings of birds in winter dusk. Of such sights, scents, and recaptured sounds is the magic of shooting.'

The obituary for the Great Shots appeared in *The Field* on 14 November 1936: 'The day of the great shots or, at any rate, of the great "professional" shots is over. No longer is it possible except for the very favoured few to pass the time from the beginning of August to the New Year in one country house after another, from moor to moor, from manor to manor.'

The glamour of the Great Shots is to some extent matched by the appeal which shooting has had for the Royal Family since the days of the Prince of Wales, later Edward VII, who after he gave up hunting took energetically to shooting. As a result, for many years, outside the shop of New Bond Street, and later at Bruton Street, Holland & Holland have been proud to give prominence to the Royal Arms and the words 'By Appointment to . . .'

The formality associated with the royal warrant is such that the following entry in Holland's Minute Book for 21 February 1911 may come as something of a surprise. 'The Secretary

The King of Portugal was an enthusiatic Holland user. Here he and the Queen visit Windsor for a shooting party in 1904. They are sitting on either side of Edward VII.

More Holland customers: the Comtesse de Paris, and King Alfonso of Spain who was shot at on his wedding day, but remained a keen sportsman nevertheless.

received from Sir William Carrington the Warrant which appointed the company Gunmakers to the King (George V). The Secretary afterwards attended at the Office of the Privy Purse and asked that the warrant might be altered to read "Gun Makers and Rifle Manufacturers to the King" and this amendment was made accordingly.'

It had been in September 1902 that Hollands were appointed gun and rifle makers to the Prince of Wales (Edward VII) and they had also supplied arms to his younger brother the Duke of Connaught, who popularised jodhpurs for riding on his return from the Durbar in India in 1902. A story is told of this Duke that when staying at Balmoral for the stalking, John Grant, the head ghilly, accompanied him. The Royal Duke missed two easy shots at stags. Grant said, 'Ye blitherin idiot! You've ruined the whole thing!'

The firm's succession of royal appointments, culminated in that of rifle makers to HRH Duke of Edinburgh, granted in 1963. The most famous of the royal shots was Edward VII and every form of shooting became a favourite pastime for him. J. E. D. Holland (later Colonel Holland) shot with him as a young man, and spoke highly of his ability, although Lord Ripon said, 'As a shot, King Edward was somewhat variable.' The fact is that he seems to have taken his sport as he found it. 'He could feel a boy's pleasure when the grouse came well to his butt, when he felt that he was shooting his best, and in fact, when everything was going right; but he was equally happy and contented when, as must often happen in Scotland, the grouse were few.'

The supply of Holland & Holland guns and rifles to members of other royal families was not of course a matter of the same warrant procedures; mention should perhaps be made of those who featured on gun case labels, including King Alfonso XIII of Spain who might have been supposed to have been put off guns, since an attempt was made to assassinate him on his wedding day in 1906. Nevertheless he came to England that same year and caused some surprise by winning the clay pigeon trophy in the Isle of Wight contest (he was also a keen sailor at Bembridge and Cowes). He shot at Windsor, and in Scotland on the Duke of Sutherland's grouse moors. King Alfonso left Spain in 1931 because of political unrest and died in exile in Rome in 1941. Appointment recognition was also held for the Kings of Sweden, Portugal and Italy and for the Czar of Russia.

A postscript on the subject of royalty. A Holland & Holland customer, Lord Lonsdale, was taunted during World War I for having had the Kaiser shooting grouse regularly on his estates at Lowther. His reply was, 'It only shows how careful one should be about picking up acquaintances when abroad.'

This stirring picture of 'A Sportswomam in India' is captioned 'With my last Barrel I fired'.

————— *11* —————

The Actual Shooting Meant Nothing

The Days of the Raj

It has been said that the British gun trade was supported by the sportsmen of India, and there are several senses in which this is true. From Birmingham came the prodigious numbers of 'export' guns, often poorly-made affairs, which went out to the East by the thousand from the middle of the 18th century. The London gunmakers, in contrast, supplied a superior type of weapon to the East India Company men, although Birmingham components may well have been used in their construction. Later, during the first twenty years or so of the 19th century, the East India Company took almost one million military arms, according to De Witt Bailey and Douglas A. Ni

Then in 1858 the British Government took over the military and administrative functions of the East India Company, and the arms issued to Indian troops were standardised. The smaller British manufacturers suffered, but the large makers of military weapons did not. We are not concerned here, of course, with guns of this type but with the superior weapons sold to the Maharajahs and to Indian soldiers for sport, and to sportsmen who made special journeys to India. But just as the East India Company supported the mass gun trade, so did the sportsmen support their London 'betters'. Famous names such as Manton became established in India as agents and, to an extent, manufacturers. To survey the kinds of weapons which firms such as Holland supplied to the Raj, it is necessary to look at the history of big game rifles, shotguns and cartridges.

For the past century and more, these weapons have traditionally been double-barrelled, and were generally made to a high standard to ensure reliability in the face of danger. Many sportsmen and those interested in firearms say double rifles are the most compelling class of firearm. Perhaps this is because these rifles have stories to tell – the scenes that they have been part of since they left the maker, the balance they may have held between life and death, and the faith that men had in them. Perhaps it is because people feel instinctively that they represent the height of the art of gunmaking. Possibly it is from an aesthetic point of view – for a best quality British double rifle with finely tapered barrels, with sidelocks, fine engraving and finely figured wood can well be said to be the 'thoroughbred' of firearms.

There have been many gunmakers but very few double rifle makers, for the complexities of making them were too great for

'Crossing the Marsemik La'. A painting by the intrepid Lady Jenkins during her solo shooting trip with her Holland gun in Tibet, 1906.

A selection of modern big game rifle cartridges from .450 3¼" to .600 Nitro Express. Beside the .600 is a .458 Winchester magnum cartridge.

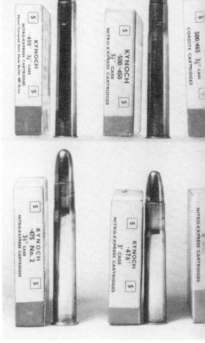

many. For a double rifle, the requirement is for a weapon giving more than five times the pressures of a shotgun, where the strength of the action and the jointing of the barrels to the action are of paramount importance to the safety of the user. The gunmaker is faced with making two barrels shoot with a 2" group at about 100 yards and where this accuracy may mean life or death to the user. These factors probably combined to inhibit many a gunmaker from embarking on the making of double rifles.

Whilst the continental countries such as Belgium, Austria and Germany have a tradition of double rifle making, the weapon is particularly associated with Britain and British gunmakers by

Close-up of Holland & Holland's 4-bore hammer rifle made for His Highness The Nizam of Hyderabad in 1885.

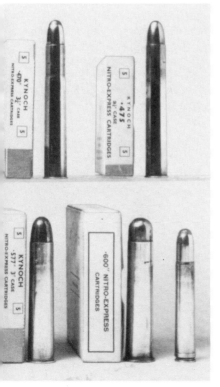

those who have shot big game or aspire to do so. This is because most of the famous big game cartridges were developed by the well-known British gun and rifle makers in conjunction with Eley Kynoch. In fact the rise of the double rifle is linked with the rise of the British Empire, and the peak period of development and manufacture was when Britain was at the zenith of its power at the beginning of the First World War.

Double rifles came into general use in the 1840s. They were made in 16 and 14 bore and a 'Best' quality London-made double rifle in those days sold for £34 – mainly for stag and boar shooting in Europe and for big game in India and Indo-China. Judging by the number of double barrel percussion rifles which have been handed down to this day, it would seem that Lancaster, Purdey and Westley Richards were among the foremost English makers of double rifles of this period. About 1865, when the first breech loaders started to be made, the calibre began to change, although the shot gun bore measurement continued to be used until the 1880s. It was during this period that the famous 8- and 4-bore double rifles were made, many of which were smooth bore, and from which the expression 'Elephant gun' arose. These large bores are particularly associated with Sir Samuel Baker, not only because he used them but because, with Gibbs of Bristol and other English rifle makers, he was closely connected with their development. They were generally smooth bore because they were only used at short ranges of up to 50 yards with spherical ball and up to that range had a lower trajectory, higher velocity and greater penetration than a weapon with rifled barrels.

Double rifles as we know them today began to appear about 1885, with the introduction of cordite and of hammerless actions. The early models were made in .303, .400, .450, .500 and .577 calibres (the last three having been very popular black powder cartridges), but were quickly followed at the close of the century by most of the famous big bore cartridges which are still in use.

Shooting was popular in India in the 1870s, without doubt, but much glamour was added to the pursuit by the publicity

given to the then Prince of Wales's tour in 1875/76. Sport was the prominent feature of it. It was written up by Sir William Howard Russell, the great Crimean correspondent. Based on his account is the following description of a visit to Jeypore, 'A surprise and wonder for ever' as Russell describes it.

'This is the threshold of the land of tigers, and it is noted that the creatures exercise a great influence over the popular imagination, as is shown by the carvings on the walls of the houses and temples. On the day after the Prince's arrival, sport was afoot. Some of the party determinedly went to resume their pig-sticking, others in quest of deer, the Prince himself being taken to a rocky ravine in which it was suspected that a tiger was lurking. His Royal Highness was placed in the upper story of a shooting box, from which he could command a view all around him, and after waiting for a couple of hours the tiger was discerned creeping towards the house. When well within range the Prince fired, apparently missing with his first barrel, but a second shot rolled the brute over. He was not fatally wounded, however, regained his feet, and crawled into some thick bush, whither the Prince was anxious to follow him on foot, but was persuaded to mount an elephant. A volley of stones drove the tiger out of the ravine, and as he walked slowly up the opposite bank, the Prince fired again. The beast had disappeared behind a

In this advertisement for the Special .577 Double Express Rifle, Holland & Holland claimed 'This sporting rifle was first made to the order of the late Sir Samuel Baker, and has received great commendation from him and most leading 'big game' sportsmen.'

With the Paradox 12-bore 'I have killed everything from tiger to snipe' said an early testimonial advertisement.

boulder, and for a few moments it was not known whether it had gone on; it had not, however, and lay dead, a full-grown tigress, eight and a half feet long.'

Russell describes how the party visited Peepul Perao, a wonderful district for jungle life with duck, teal, kingfishers, reed warblers, painted and common snipe, rails, dippers, butcher birds, partridge and quail; parrots, many sorts of thrush or grackles, woodpeckers, fly-catchers, owls; jungle cock in the thick stuff, black partridge on the outskirts, and porcupines rattling over the dry watercourses; hares near the cultivated patches; by the edges of the woods little burrowing creatures like marmosets. Above all career eagles, falcons, hawks, buzzards and kites. But these were left unmolested, the quarry being tiger, and the sound of shooting, had guns been fired at insignificant game, would probably have driven away any of these beasts that might be in the immediate neighbourhood. 'The camp must have resembled a species of town. It contained 2500 persons, exclusive of General Ramsay's separate establishment; there were 119 elephants, 550 camels, 100 horses, 60 carts drawn by oxen, many goats and milch cows, 600 coolies, 60 tent-pitchers, 20 water-carriers, 40 messengers and attendants, 75 non-commissioned officers and men of the 3rd Gurkhas and their band, troopers of the Bengal Cavalry and Native Infantry, together with mahouts, camel-men, and the Europeans. The Prince's person was exclusively guarded by natives.' 'Certainly,' Sir William says, 'I should feel rather proud of myself if I were a wild beast and knew all this.'

In the period up to 1914 the British double rifle makers, such as Rigby, Holland & Holland, Westley Richards and Jeffery vied with each other to produce new cartridges to promote the sale of their products – just as the American manufacturers of single barrel rifles have been doing during the past 25 years or more. For example, in that pre-First World War period no less than eleven large bore cartridges were introduced, from the .450 Nitro Express up to the .500 3¼". Nine of these were of more or less the same ballistics – throwing a bullet of between 480 and 520 grains.

It was during this period too that the .375 Holland & Holland Magnum was introduced. The belted rimless version of this cartridge, which is widely regarded as the best all-round rifle cartridge in the world, was introduced in 1911, and the first double rifle chambered for the flanged version of this cartridge was introduced shortly after the war.

The production of the .300 H & H Magnum belted rimless cartridge was held up by the First World War, and this cartridge was not put into production until 1919. Its flanged version for double rifles was introduced in 1925. From then on and up to World War II, there was no further development of big or medium bore double rifle cartridges. Instead the trend went the other way with the introduction of a number of flanged varieties of small bores such as the .240 and .275 or 7mm.

To return to the early part of the twentieth century, it was also during this period that the great Indian Princes were competing with each other to have the finest armoury of high-quality weapons, and after the First World War this competition increased, and whole series of weapons were sent not only to dealers in India such as Walter Locke & Co., Manton's, Lyon and Lyon, and R. B. Rodda, but also directly to the Rulers them-

RIGHT: His Excellency the Governor of Madras (centre) and a party of 25 guns, shot some 850 duck at Parlakemidi in 1926.

This picture of the Prince of Wales's elephant charged by a tiger was published in 1876. But pictures of elephants being so attacked are common, perhaps more imaginative than documentary.

BELOW: *HH the Maharajah of Cooch Behar described Holland & Holland's rifles as 'admirable weapons. I killed a bull bison with one of them with a single shot at 80 yards'.*

selves, and the names of the Maharajas of Bikaner, Jodhpur, Surguja, Barwani, Rewa, Mysore, Kapurthala, Patiala and many others appear frequently in Holland's ledgers. Many of these weapons were highly engraved, inlaid with ivory and precious metals and some had enamel work applied. Even the cases in which they were fitted were often of extraordinary quality, many being of crocodile skin, with silver mounts and fittings. The finest armouries probably belonged to the Nawab of Bhopal and the Maharajas of Alwar and Patiala. The Maharajah of Alwar was a strict Hindu, and would have no article of cowhide on any of his weapons, so the face-pads were supplied with sponge-rubber inserts, and the cases were either of oak or were canvas-covered.

'Up to the 1920s, the countryside was teeming with game. Along the road you could shoot peafowl, deer, partridge –anything. Of course, later it got shot out.' So reports an English resident in India. 'More than once we got bags of more than a thousand duck a day with eight guns,' reports another. The attitude was, 'there was so much game that there was no harm in it.' On viceregal and princely shoots, where game was 'slain literally by the hundreds' and scores were kept to compare one viceroy with an earlier occupant, trophy hunting and killing were gradually being replaced by a more natural philosophy 'It was in stalking and in hunting that you had your fun. The actual shooting meant nothing really. The only thing was to kill outright.'

It was an age in India of almost unlimited shooting for the Rulers in their private preserves – when, for example, the late Maharaja of Surguja could boast at the end of his life that he had killed 1,600 tigers. It was an age too when there was equally unlimited shooting for the British civil administration

and for Army officers. Many of them probably could not afford a 'Best' London made double rifle when they started their service, and instead were content with cheaper model Anson & Deeley or boxlock double rifles. These were made as a rule in Birmingham and bore many famous names like William Evans, Tolley and Boswell, as well as the Army & Navy Stores – the last port of call for hundreds of men before they left for India, Malaya, Burma or for the African colonies. There can be no finer recommendation for these cheaper British double rifles than the fact that large numbers of them are still in use today, with battered stocks but with barrels as tight on the actions as the day they were first sold.

Since the end of the Second World War, Eley Kynoch, the only makers of big bore flanged ammunition in the world, had gradually had to phase out production of these cartridges. Such calibres as the .476 Westley Richards, the .475 No. 2 Jeffery and the .500/450 Holland & Holland were discontinued. Others disappeared during the 1950s, until in 1967 the Eley Kynoch factory decided to cease manufacture of all flanged metallic cartridges. This decision had become inevitable for the annual sales of such famous cartridges as the .470 and the .500/465 have now been reduced to a few thousand per year. The fall in demand is due to several reasons. Firstly, the very restricted imports of ammunition into India since the handing over of power by the British in 1947, coupled with the fact that the plains and forest game of India is rapidly approaching extinction. Secondly, in Africa from 1900 to 1939, almost every European settler, who was keen on shooting, owned a double rifle. Now that the game is less and so many of the settlers in the former colonies have left, the ownership of the double rifle is restricted to the professional hunters and to the few sportsmen going on safari.

One of the keenest shots of all the Viceroys was Lord Curzon, seen here standing up in his howdah to discuss tactics with a neighbouring howdah.

PREVIOUS PAGE:

When the Illustrated London News *printed this picture by F T Daws, which was exhibited at the Royal Academy, they captioned it as follows: Tiger-shooting in India is traditionally a royal sport, of which both the King and the Prince of Wales have had experience. The painting here reproduced illustrates the occasion on which the Prince shot his first tiger, in December 1921, in the jungles of Nepal. He was the guest of the Maharajah Sir Chandra Shumshere Jung, and was accompanied by Lord Louis Mountbatten, Lord Cromer, Sir Lionel Halsey, and Colonel Worgan. On the first of four days' sport, the total bag was eleven tigers and two rhinoceros.*

When Britain handed over power in India in 1947 the country was teeming with big game - tiger especially. The big game was preserved either by the former Indian rulers or, in British India, by the strict regulation of licences in the so-called blocks in the reserve forests. Most of the shooting was done by the rulers, princes, and by officers of the Indian and British Army or civilian administrators, and when the hand-over of power took place there was an estimated tiger population of well over 50,000. Today it is estimated at about 2,500.

By the early 1950s, many companies and individuals in India blossomed forth as *shikari* (*shikar* is the Persian word for shooting) outfitters, on the lines of the African safari companies. They built up considerable businesses which brought in large amounts of foreign exchange, but the big game of India has been decimated and most of these firms are today out of business. The destruction of the forest game has been due to the almost unrestricted issue of firearms licences, to poaching at night, to poisoning, and, finally and most important, to the destruction of habitat – the cutting down of the jungles for firewood.

Sanctuaries have been created but they are mostly sanctuaries in name only – even if there are no villages in them, the villagers from outside are allowed to graze their cattle, sheep and goats within the area – to the detriment of the feed for the herbivorous wild game. It is difficult to commercialize the wild life of India for viewing and photography, simply because so much of the plains game are forest-living animals, and are difficult to find and to see.

The big game of the mountains of India, which used to be so

A vivid contrast with the earlier royal visit to India was in 1961 when Queen Elizabeth and the Duke of Edinburgh attended a rhino shoot.

highly prized by enthusiastic British sportsmen who were prepared to undergo great hardships to shoot these wild sheep and goats of the Himalayas, now lie in restricted areas along the Himalayan range. These are virtually inaccessible to all but the Indian Army on the borders against China – and the Indian Army have themselves destroyed much of this unique fauna. Fortunately, there are kingdoms like Nepal and Bhutan where the rulers are keen sportsmen and conservationists and where the mountain game is preserved.

A number of countries in Asia have come to realize the great value of big game hunting as an earner of foreign exchange.

In Afghanistan, the Government had, before the Russian invasion, been issuing licences to a limited number of people each summer to go to the southern part of the Pamirs (which lie just in Afghanistan in the Wakhan) to shoot an ovis poli, the huge sheep named after Marco Polo, who first recorded it. A licence to shoot one cost £2,500 and the total cost of the trip amounted to £4,500 – and that was back in 1970.

Even the governments of the Soviet Union and the Mongolian People's Republic appreciate the value of foreign exchange to be earned from their big game and very expensive licences are obtainable to shoot red deer and bear in Russia, and the Mongolian wild sheep. But it was India which captured the imagination of those who only shot tigers from the arm chair in their club, and it was India in the days of the Raj which will long be remembered as the place where the actual shooting meant everything.

Holland & Holland reproduced this picture of a stamp in 1907, saying that seven consecutive shots at 100 yards would have struck a postage stamp. 'The group illustrated was made with the 480 grain bullet as fired from the .465 cartridge. It was produced at the very first attempt, and it constitutes what seems likely to stand for some time to come as a record amongst properly authenticated targets. The centres of the whole seven shots lie within a space practically 1 in. square (actually 1.00 in. by 1.05 in.), and the reader may satisfy himself from the reproduction of part of the actual target that all the shots would have hit a postage stamp. It is interesting to know that the sights used were of the open variety, and that orthoptic spectacles were not employed.

The bullet which produced these remarkable results, in conjunction with the cartridge and rifle under review, has been appropriately christened 'Velopex'.

As regards the ballistics of the cartridge, Holland & Holland have always aimed at a low chamber pressure, believing this to be necessary in view of the conditions under which sporting rifles are used in tropical climates. The rifle used was a .465-bore Express Cordite Rifle.

'Flooring the Elephant in Africa'

Big Game Hunting

This picture was used in an advertisement for the 10-bore Paradox ideal for shooting elephant, bison and other kinds of large game such as the rhinoceros. Lord Wolverton, writing in Five Months in Somaliland *from which the picture is taken, is observing 'Coming suddenly on the rhino, I fired at his heart, knocking him over on the spot'.*

The hunting of big game is an ancient and honourable sport dating back several thousand years in Asia and parts of North Africa, and at least a thousand years in Europe. It has always been the sport of the rich – rulers, princes and noblemen – and even today a licence to shoot one animal can cost at least £2000.

Most people associate big game with Central Africa but in fact it is a comparatively modern sport here developed during the past 100 years. The early settlers and administrators in Central, East and Southern Africa found a country with what appeared unlimited wild animals. They hunted big game for meat and for sport. And many species of these animals in Africa are named after people who first recorded them even as recently as 60 years ago.

From these early days, the hunters required specially-made guns and rifles to follow their quarry. When double rifles were first produced in the early part of the 19th century their *raison d'être* was greater fire power, and the introduction of repeating rifles might have led to their disappearance. However, the

early European hunters who went to Africa came to realise the great advantage of a double rifle over a repeating rifle – namely safety. Here was a weapon with two barrels and two lock mechanisms and these offered the best insurance against death or injury. Hence the double rifle became, and remains to this day, the accepted weapon for use against dangerous game.

Big game hunting in Africa expanded, the right guns were available and other factors like the coming of the railways in the 1880s and 1890s were of great significance. Not only did they enable the British to conduct a safari in a matter of weeks instead of months – or months instead of years – they encouraged rich Americans and others from far afield. Probably the most famous of these was 'Teddy' Roosevelt, former President of the USA, and user of a Holland & Holland rifle.

Theodore Roosevelt had been President of the United States for eight years and had previously been Vice President, when he retired at 50 years old. He was to die eleven years later. 'From childhood to death he was engaged in a continual struggle to overcome physical infirmities, family misfortunes and political crises'. Instead of taking a well-deserved rest, as a retirement present to himself, he chose to make for the 'African Game Trials' as he called them in his book, published in 1910. He spent altogether a year in Africa, with his son Kermit, on a tour, the arrangements for which 'had chiefly been made

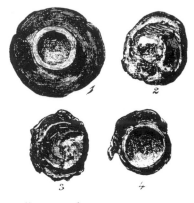

Bullets 1 and 2 were cut out of tigers shot by Sir Samuel Baker, and No 3 and 4 were from grizzly bears.

The Princess Hélène d'Orleans, a Holland customer, toured Africa in 1910 and is seen here with a hippo she shot at Buzi, then in Portuguese East Africa.

Ostrich hunting somewhere in Africa, was indulged in both for the feathers and food.

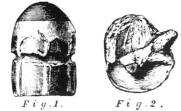

Fig. 1. Fig. 2.

Fig. 1. 8-bore 'Paradox' steel cored bullet, of which Captain Swayne said 'The bullet had passed obliquely through the rhinoceros, and was found under the skin on the other side.' Fig. 2. 8-bore 'Paradox' hardened solid bullet, fired at rhinoceros. 'Entered at one side and came out at top of opposite shoulder.'

through two valued English friends, Mr Frederick Courtenay Selous, the greatest of the world's big-game hunters, and Mr Edward North Buxton, also a mighty hunter.'

Buxton, as a mark of friendship from England to a distinguished President, sent him a double-barrel .500–.450 Holland. (He also took on the expedition an army 30 calibre Springfield and a Winchester .405.) Work had begun on it in 1908 and it was 'best quality .450 bore royal grade'. The gun was made with a gold circular inlay on the butt, engraved with the Presidential eagle and the inscription TR/1909.

Roosevelt's foreword to his book is somewhat lyrical:

'I speak of Africa and golden joys: the joy of wandering through lonely lands; the joy of hunting the mighty and terrible lords of the wilderness; the cunning, the wary and the grim . . . The land teems with beasts of the chase infinite in number and incredible in variety (he was to capture and identify 1100 species). It holds the fiercest beasts of ravin, and the fleetest and most timid of those things that live in undying fear of talon and fang . . . These things can be told. But there are no words that can tell the hidden spirit of the wilderness.'

Powerful stuff, but Roosevelt was much more specific when it came to talking about his Holland and big game shooting. His first bull rhino convinced him that 'the vitality of the huge pachyderm was so great, its mere bulk counted for so much, that even such a hard-hitting rifle as my double Holland – than which I do not believe there exists a better weapon for heavy game – could not stop it outright, although either of the wounds inflicted would have been fatal in a few seconds.'

Of another rhino he says, after making 'a tolerably fair comparison between his Winchester and the Holland for heavy game like rhinos and buffaloes, I found that for me personally, the heavy Holland was unquestionably the proper weapon'. And, later, 'I was confirmed in my judgement that for me personally the big Holland rifle was the only weapon, although I did not care as much for it against lighter-bodied beasts like lions'. Of course, the big Holland was a tough weapon to handle. 'The recoil of the heavy rifle made me rock,' he writes, 'as I stood unsteadily on my perch, and I failed to hit the brain. But the bullet, only missing the brain by an inch or two, brought the elephant to its knees; as it rose, I floored it with the second barrel. The blast of the big barrel, by the way, was none too pleasant for the other men on the logs, and made Cunninghame's nose bleed.' He concludes that although the Winchester and the Springfield were good weapons for elephants, 'I kept to my belief that, for such very heavy game, my Holland was an even better weapon'.

The safari was, says his biographer, the 'great moment of his private life'.

The gunmaker and historian W. W. Greener concludes that 'To slay so ponderous an animal as a full-grown elephant, a weapon is required that will give good penetration with great smashing and paralysing power. Ordinary rifles are useless as the bullets smash up long before they reach the vital organ. An 8-bore or 4-bore will give excellent penetration and the paralysing power of the bullet crushing through the body will invariably drop an elephant, even when charging. 'Often nothing but the immediate flooring of the elephant will save the life of the sportsman and his attendants, and an 8-bore will frequently fail to stop the charge.' Holland made just such a gun, and, as we heard earlier, Henry Holland himself worked on

Teddy Roosevelt's safari fording a river.

Fig. 3.

8-bore 'Paradox' steel cored bullet, taken out of bull elephant. Mr Digly Davies writes: 'Bull elephant shot at 25 yards. Shot through the shoulder and found sticking in the skin on the opposite side. Animal dropped dead on the spot.'

Samual Baker's big gun when he was an apprentice. This gun was the famous 'Baby', a single barrelled rifle which weighed 20 lb and fired a charge of 10 drachms of powder behind a half-pound shell. Baker took 'Baby' (as well as Lady Baker) on an African expedition in 1871, working his way across the Sudan and down the Nile to Lake Albert. The gun was an object of awe to the local population, and the Arabs named it *Jenna el Mootfah* (child of a cannon) and he claimed that he never fired a shot from it without getting his animal. He described his adventures in a book which was largely responsible for popularising big game shooting in Africa.

Sir Samuel Baker's first book *The Rifle and Hound in Ceylon* had been moderately successful, but his next, published in 1866, had acquired for him the reputation of the mighty hunter. This was *Albert N'Yanza, Great Basin of the Nile*, dedicated to Queen Victoria. On the expedition he described, he had carried a powerful pair of No. 10 polygroove rifles made by Reilly of Oxford Street. But he required something more powerful to deal with elephants and the like, hence 'Baby' described in the next book, *The Nile Tributaries of Abyssinia*. This is full of information about hunting elephants, buffaloes, rhinoceros and lions, for which purpose he carried ten guns, including a single rifle by Manton. Actually, Baker was a serious explorer, holding the Gold Medal of the Royal Geographical Society, who averred 'my pleasure is not in slaughtering . . . but to restrict my shooting only to specimen heads.' In his 1874 book *Ismailia* a narrative of the expedition to Central Africa for the suppression of the slave trade, he describes in detail how he shot elephant along the Nile, although he says, 'I should have thought it almost as likely to meet a herd of elephants in Hyde Park as to find them in this open and thickly populated country.' He rose to the occasion, observing: 'I always kept my guns and ammunition in beautiful order, arranged in a rack in the cabin. These included two Holland half-pounders, that carried an iron lead-coated explosive shell, containing a bursting charge of half an ounce of fine grain powder. The two elephant rifles were very hard hitters and carried twelve drachms of powder.' When he fired at his first elephant, the gun 'by the recoil flew out of my hands for a distance of 12 yards'.

'The rifles were the same calibre and pattern as "the Baby" and made by Mr Holland of Bond Street, and are the most overpowering rifles I ever used. They were certain to kill the elephant, and to half kill the man who fired them . . . I was tolerably strong, therefore I was never killed outright, but an Arab hunter had his collar bone smashed by the recoil.' Baker ran out of ammunition after he had killed two of the ten elephants in the herd.

Books like these were an eye-opener to the better-off British shot, bored with beak and feather, and looking for something on a larger scale. The White Hunter and the professional safari were born, with the British playing the leading rôle for the next 60 years. But the better-off, or the really well-off, were joined or succeeded by the less well-off, as an article in *The Field* described in truly prophetic words in 1935. Of all sports, said *The Field*

'none has been more changed by modern inventions than big game shooting. Putting aside the immense advance in

Theodore Roosevelt and one of his big lions. The photograph was taken by his son.

Sir Samuel Baker's 'Baby' made by Henry Holland. It was trodden on by an elephant and repaired by elephant skin sheathed round the hand and action.

sporting rifles of the past thirty, indeed of the past ten years, there are two factors that have influenced it in the realms of scientific invention – the perfection of the camera, and especially the cine-camera, and the internal combustion engine . . . The use of the motor car was at one time vilely abused in Africa by using it as a mobile butt. That is a thing of the past . . . the motor car is welcomed as an integral part of shooting from Cape to Cairo by sportsmen of the best type. It represents an immense saving in time, generally a considerable saving in money, and, most important of all, it removes so much of the difficulties of organisation required in a porter safari . . . But the factor that has chiefly revolutionised shooting is the aeroplane.'

The writer foresaw 'an enormous increase in the number of people who will fly abroad to see, to photograph or to shoot big game'.

This revolution came about because there were plenty of well-off people who habitually went up to Scotland for six weeks or two months' holiday, spending a few hundred pounds on a shooting holiday, who now, thanks to Imperial Airways, found Africa to be within their time scale. This was true, too, for the Americans.

In the past 25 years most of the safari business has come from the United States, with, a long way behind, Italians, Mexicans and wealthy South Americans.

The cost of a safari in, say, Kenya today for one person for a month will come to about £80,000, and most of the safari companies in the former European colonies in Africa have a waiting list of up to two years. Most of the new African self-governing nations realise the tremendous economic value of the big game and are taking every measure possible to preserve the national parks for sightseers and photographers and the hunting areas for shooting.

To those who have never seen big game in the wild and who have seen wild animals only in zoos or on films, the case for shooting them may appear indefensible. The sportsman and naturalist, the late Colonel Richard Meinertzhagen, wrote in his big game hunting record book in 1946:

'This is a record of slaughter for which there is little excuse. Much was shot for food; it gave me good healthy exercise, it

taught me bushcraft and how to shoot straight. But was the cost of life worth it? I now have little to show for it and am not in the least proud of it. When I was young I had the hunting instinct strongly developed. That was satisfied to the full, but I now repent.'

One can understand what he meant. He had hunted between 75 and 100 years ago when the game appeared almost limitless. He wrote the words long before the World Wild Life Fund had come into being, and long before big game shooting had become almost a nasty word to mention in Britain.

Nevertheless, 'shooters' of big game are the greatest conservationists, and even though today they may not all be 'hunters' they do contribute either by what they pay or in other ways to the conservation of the game. In this connexion it is worth remembering that many species of Indian game especially, and some African species, have been introduced into large private ranches in parts of North and South America – albeit for sport – but where the climate suits them and where in a few years they may be the only ones of their kind left apart from those in zoos.

The 1920s and 1930s were the years of the 'White Hunter' and we know much about him, thanks to the films and books by the likes of Ernest Hemingway and Ruark.

The year 1945 marked the watershed of big-game shooting in Africa, with a number of countries becoming independent in the following years, and closing their borders, at least for a time, to the hunters. To mark the end of an era, Holland produced, during the 1970s, the last .600 bore double rifle using nitro cartridges.

The .600 bore Nitro Express was the most powerful sporting rifle and cartridge ever produced in Britain. It was not derived from a Black Powder version, and there is no information on who designed the cartridge. However, it is known that W. J. Jeffery (a subsidiary company of Holland & Holland) was the first to produce these rifles, and there is a relevant note in the first page of the Jeffery number book commencing 1901 which says '23/3/01 Thro' Bakers—4 pairs .600 bore tubes from Krupps @75/- per pair.'

The first Jeffery .600 bore double rifle, No 12175, was an 'under snap' Anson & Deeley action rifle, and weighed 15lb 10oz. It was finished in February 1902 and sold for £45. One of the first big game hunters to acquire a Jeffery .600 bore double rifle was Major P. H. G. Powell-Cotton, who describes it in his book *Unknown Africa*. He also mentions the calibre in the appendices of his earlier book *A Sporting Trip through Abyssinia* published in 1902. He recommends it as 'taking the place of the 8B'. Probably he saw, and possibly tried out, a .600 bore when he returned to England at the end of 1901. John Taylor also mentions in *African Rifles and Cartridges* that he owned one. A number of .600 bores of different makes were to be found in the armouries of the Indian Princes, and most of these rifles were in completely unused condition. The last one of the thirty-two double barrel .600 bores made by Jeffery was sold in 1929. In addition, the Company made twenty-four single barrel .600 bores, a few on Anson & Deeley actions, but the majority of falling block Farquharson actions. One of the latter is in a collection in Fort Worth and was used as an

In Sir Samuel Baker's Wild Beasts and Their Ways *he wrote 'My battery is one .577, one .400 and one 'Magnum Paradox,' No 12. The 'Paradox' is a most useful weapon, as it combines a shot gun (shoots No 6 shot with equal pattern to a best cylinder-bored gun) with a rifle that is wonderfully accurate within a range of 100 yards.'*

'No. 1. – Struck a large Barra Singha deer upon the spine, and the bullet was found embedded in crushed bone.'

No. 2. – Passed behind the shoulder of a full-grown bear, and struck the bone of another bear below the shoulder joint, a few paces on the other side of the first wounded animal.'

'No. 3. – This went through a bear, and was found beneath the skin upon the opposite side.'

'The Last .600-Bore Double Rifle' left lock.

. . . and right lock.

. . . and underside.

armament on a British vessel during the First World War.

A few .600 bore double rifles were made by other British makers – three by Westley Richards; nine by Wilkes – but Mr Tom Wilkes remembers his father saying that the firm made quite a number for the trade – possibly for firms like the Army and Navy Stores. Curiously, one of Britain's most famous makers of double rifles, John Rigby, says there is no record of their having made a .600 bore. The Holland & Holland records show six 'Royal' Model .600 bores as having been made by the Company, and Purdey's have made the same number. Some too were made in Belgium, but it is doubtful if any were made elsewhere on the Continent. So, in all it is possible that about seventy-five .600 bore double rifles were made, which means that with the single barrel rifles made by Jeffery and some other makers, notably P. Webley, the total number of .600 bore rifles of all kinds which have ever been made would only slightly exceed one hundred.

The Kynoch records show that the first commercial batch of .600 cartridges were loaded in 1901. The Kynoch cartridges were available with 100 grains of powder – either Cordite at £23.00 per 1,000 or Axite at £28.15.0 per 1,000 (today, ten of these cartridges would be worth those prices, or more). Eley Brothers also made the .600 bore cartridge until 1918. An amalgamation then took place of all the explosive manufacturers in Britain, which was called Explosives Trades Limited for a few months until they re-christened themselves Nobel Industries in November 1918. From then on all .600 bore cartridges were head-stamped 'Kynoch', although strangely enough Kynoch was the smallest of the five explosive manufacturers who had amalgamated.

In later years the standard .600 cartridge was loaded with 110 grains of powder only. John Taylor in *African Rifles and Cartridges* says that all Jeffery rifles were sighted for the 100 grain powder load. This is not so. Latterly they were mainly 110 grains loads, and there is one Jeffery rifle recorded – No 12431 – made in 1902 which weighed 12½lb and was sighted in for a 120 grain powder load.

The .600 bore cartridge remained in current production until 1956, when the last batch of 2,000 cartridges was loaded by IMI (Kynoch) for Holland & Holland. During the fifty years of manufacture IMI (Kynoch) believe that as many as 200,000 cartridges were made, and say that after the Second World War several batches, each of 15/20,000 cartridges, were made. If 200,000 is correct, this means an average of 2,000 cartridges per rifle. Where they went and what happened to them is a mystery, for it is hardly credible that much more than 10 per cent were ever used.

The 'Last .600 Bore Rifle', which is probably the finest Holland & Holland double rifle ever made, was started in 1970 when the barrels were made by Mr David Winks in the Holland & Holland barrel shop. The finishing touches were made almost exactly five years later, just after Easter 1975. It is not possible to say exactly the number of hours which went into the design, thought and manufacture of the rifle by the craftsmen of Holland & Holland and its case, but it certainly runs into many thousands. During this time, the rifle was worked upon by almost all of the best craftsmen at Holland &

Holland under the personal supervision of Mr Geoffrey Brooks the Production Director.

It was decided to embellish the rifle by portraying some of the people, some of the fauna and some of the flora of Africa. A well known sculptor and artist made pencil drawings of the animal scenes which are engraved on the rifle, and a folio containing these original drawings accompanies the rifle. The magnificient portrayal of these and other scenes was sculpted by Mr Kenneth Hunt, in a unique style never before applied to a breech-loading British sporting gun or rifle. The very open scenes in high relief do not use heavy shading usually applied in relief engraving on firearms.

This beautiful weapon, The Last .600 Bore, is a fitting tribute to a sport where the camera has now replaced the rifle.

13

'Half an Inch of Plank between Himself and Eternity'

The Punt Gunner 1850–1890

A professional wildfowler wore his sacking suit for camouflage and protection.

Few of the professional punt gunners of the nineteenth century have left much literature behind themselves, but we do know something of what their life might have been like from a remarkable account by Brian Jackman who found records of a Yorkshire punt gunner who died in 1913. 'The guns are silent now,' wrote Jackman.

'The armoury has been dispersed and the old man in his grave for more than half a century. But the legend of Snowden Slights, last of the Yorkshire wildfowlers, still lingers in the Derwent valley.

'By a strange twist of history his old killing ground, a wild waste of flooded water-meadow called Wheldrake Ings, is now a nature reserve where wintering wildfowl are strictly protected. The Yorkshire Derwent is one of the last great unspoiled lowland rivers of northern England and the broad reaches around Wheldrake have not altered much since the days of Snowden Slights. Pictures taken around the turn of the century reveal Snowden as a great, gaunt oak of a man, his face deep-etched and pinched by the hard marsh winters.

'He was born in 1830, when wildfowling with punt and gun was still quite new to the Derwent. By the time he was nine he had already left school to join his father on regular punt-gunning forays. By the time he was 15 he was a dead shot, a hefty, big-boned lad who thought nothing of walking to Pocklington market twice a week with a sack of dead ducks – a round of 18 miles.

'In summer he worked as a basket-weaver, and when he married he sank all his small capital in an osier bed to grow the supple willows which are the raw materials of the basket-maker's trade. But soon afterwards, disaster struck. A freak winter destroyed his osiers and left him penniless. Fortunately the ice and floods which had brought him ruin also provided his salvation. Huge flocks of wildfowl came pouring out of the sky like snowflakes to settle among the drowning fields; wild swans from Russia, baying packs of geese from the frozen east coast estuaries and all kinds of duck. Everyday during that terrible freeze he lay in his low grey punt, the hoar frost crusted on his corduroy coat, creeping like an old dog otter across the misty waters. And every day his great muzzle-loading punt gun boomed out

over the fen, drenching the huddled flocks with its deadly leaden blizzard. And so he not only kept himself and his family from starvation but also found himself on the road to becoming the king of the Yorkshire punt-gunners.

'Sculling the Fowl in a Calm Sea' from Payne-Gallwey's book.

'Those were the days when anything that flew was fair game, and Snowden laid into the local wildfowl with a determination that would have appalled present-day bird-lovers. You could buy a plump pinkfoot goose for 3s. 6d. Bitterns were 2 shillings each, kingfishers 1 shilling, a jack snipe sixpence. Once he was within 35 yards of his target he seldom missed. He once hit 24 mallard and 20 widgeon with one shot, although that doesn't seem quite so remarkable when you look at the artillery he used. Some of his guns had barrels as big as drainpipes. His biggest one, a giant muzzle-loader built in Beverley for his father, weighed 140lb and had a barrel 10ft long that could throw 16oz of lead. These formidable old goose guns he mounted in an open clinker-built pinewood punt 17ft long with a 3ft beam. When fully laden with gun and gunner the gunwales cleared the water by a mere six inches.

'He was still wildfowling when he was 80, two years before his death in 1913. His had been a tough and solitary life, lying for hours on end in his punt, often soaked, frequently frozen (once he was found with his corduroys frozen on him and carried home, stiff as a board, to be thawed out by his fireside). Yet he is on record as having said: "If I had my life to come over again I would be a wildfowler, but I would go in for it properly." God help the geese if he had, says Jackman.'

Amateur fowling is much more widely described, and by none more enthusiastically than the prince of punt-gunners, Sir Ralph Payne-Gallwey Bt, author of *The Fowler in Ireland*. He tells us that the punt gunners 'used their "big guns" in calmer weather, when great rafts of wildfowl would gather in an estuary, or in the lee of a spit of land, or on a sandbank. On any day's outing, they did not usually fire more than one shot, and that only after careful stalking and manoeuvring to close with the birds. Many days were "blank" days owing to an unsuccessful stalk or a freshening of the weather, the latter possibly causing danger to the gunner, as the gunwales of the punts were very close to the water.

'The punts which were specially built for gunning were long with wide, flat bottoms for shallow draught. They were enclosed by decking with an opening for the gunner, and had to be stoutly built to resist the effects of recoil when the gun was fired. When making the approach to fowl, smaller punts were usually paddled, but the larger double-handed punts were often propelled by sculling: this was quieter, enabled the profile of the gunner to be kept at a minimum and the movement took place toward the stern of the punt, out of the line of sight of the waterfowl which were being approached.'

Punt guns were originally muzzle-loaders, but in the mid-19th century were being converted or built as breech-loaders, probably on the Snider system to begin with (though Thomas Bland produced a 'new' punt gun on the Snider principle as late as 1882). The years from 1850 to 1890 constituted the high period of punt-gunning, and many gunmakers produced new guns on their own systems. Among the most successful of these was Holland & Holland's 'London' punt gun, which was illustrated and reviewed in *The Field* late in 1879. This was generally made in 1½" bore, though 1⅜", 1¾" and 2" bore guns

The No 1 gun of the Set of Six Wildfowl and Wader Guns 1983. A Magnum 12-bore.

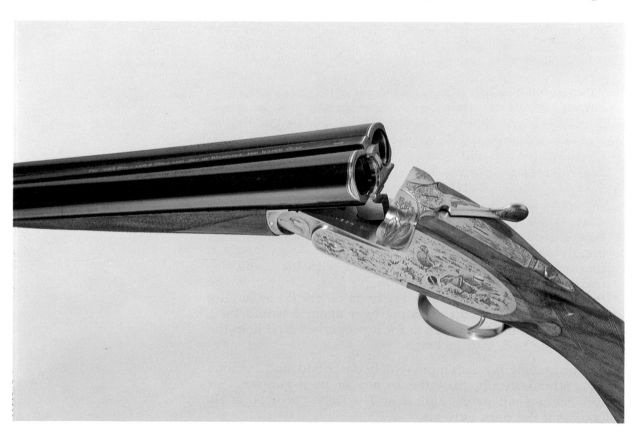

The stalking horse nearly out of its depth.

were also made. The 1½" gun usually had a 8' 6" barrel, weighed around 100lb, and fired between 16 and 32ozs of shot.

One of the greatest problems with which the punt-gunner had to contend was recoil. With a heavy gun firing a relatively light load the problem was greatly reduced, and some gunners used no breeching ropes or other recoil apparatus, but took the recoil on their chest. This could be very dangerous, however, if for any reason there was excessive recoil and in January 1881 the death was reported of a punt-gunner Mr Robert Pooly, who was killed by the recoil of his gun on his chest. Subsequent investigation proved that his gun had been loaded for some time, and the shot and wadding had become damp, causing the excessive recoil which killed Mr Pooly.

Many systems were devised to absorb the recoil of the big gun, but perhaps the most popular was Col. Peter Hawker's system.

Very little is known about the performance of the Holland gun, known as the 'London'; hence the interest in the following description published in 1884 by Mr J. H. Walsh:

'This firm appears to have succeeded in throwing all their competitors into the shade by the invention of their new punt gun some few years ago, which they have appropriately named "The London", as it is really invented, bored and actioned in the metropolis, being, I believe, the only instance of gun barrel boring at present carried on out of Birmingham. At first their barrels were made of iron, but the firm have at length succeeded in making them out of steel, which is of that description termed "mild", and is made in Sheffield and sent up to London in a solid block. The barrel

A contemporary engraving of the 'London' Punt Gun with (below right) Mr. E. T. Booth's Recoil Box and (below left) the bars for locking the extractor.

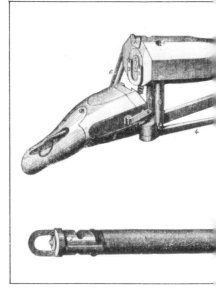

is then bored out of the solid, and the gun actioned and made in London.

'The advantages claimed for a steel barrel are, firstly, its increased strength and lightness; and, secondly, its giving better shooting, both in regularity and closeness of pattern and increased penetration. It was always very difficult to get the iron barrels free from flaws, and, in consequence of the difficulty in "setting" them after they were welded, they were very rarely really straight; hence the complaints often made of their not shooting as regularly and as "hard" as they should have done. The steel barrels, on the other hand are drilled from the solid in a particular manner with very powerful machinery, and are perfectly straight; and those shown to me by Messrs. Holland had a polish inside like that in a highly finished 12-bore gun.

'*1st. As to safety:*

The breech-action is constructed so that no part of the recoil comes upon the stock at all, but is taken up by the two steel rods which shut up through half-round slots, one on each side of the extractor, the other halves being cut in the breech end of the gun, so that all the strain comes eventually upon the breech of the gun-barrel itself.

'As a test of the great strength of the action, I am told that the guns are sent to the proof-house in the finished state, so that the actions as they are when used by sportsman stand first and second proof. But the mechanism proves itself.

'Messrs. Holland showed me two very large guns, 2in bore, which they had just proved; one was for use in the bow of a steam launch, and the other was for a double-handed punt. They had both stood the following heavy charges, and were proof-marked accordingly:

1st Proof. Charge, 18¾oz powder, 26oz lead plug.

2nd Proof. Charge, 13½oz powder, 26oz lead plug.

'The breech end of the gun is made very stout at its extreme end; this is not so much for safety as absorb recoil, and also has the advantage of causing the gun to balance well out board, and thus gives the punter more room in the punt.

'*2nd. Shooting Powers:*

Perhaps no better test of the shooting powers of the "London" could be referred to than the trial made by Mr E. T. Booth, some two years ago; the results were published in the columns of *The Field* at the time. Mr Booth had a favourite muzzle-loading 1½" gun, which he had always considered a remarkably hard and close shooting one, and with which he had beaten many other guns, muzzle- and breech-loading, of the same bore.

'This gun was pitted against one of Holland's 1½" "London" guns, and the trial was carried out by Mr Booth himself, the guns being shot side by side at the same time, and loaded by Mr Booth with the same charges. Range 100yds; target of wood. In the result the breech-loader beat the muzzle-loader, both in pattern and penetration, by about 12 or 15 per cent. This trial clearly shows that there is no reason excepting faulty construction, why a breech-loader should not shoot as well as or even better than a muzzle-loader.

'*3rd Ease of Loading:*

The action of the "London" is very simple. The lever being turned to the right, the stocks falls and exposes the face of the breech end of the barrel. The cartridge being placed in the clips of the extractor is pushed into the barrel, the stock is then lifted up, and the lever turned home when the gun is ready for firing.

'*4th Extraction:*

Is simple and certainly effective. Usually the empty case can be easily pulled out by the extractor, but should it stick, the head of the extractor (which has a strong quick thread upon it) can be turned, and this brings the empty cartridge out about half an inch and relieves the case, so that it can be drawn out with one finger.'

Very little was actually known about the practical performance of the guns. One test was carried out by a *Field* correspondent

Shooting wild duck on the Potomac in the USA about 1850.

A most interesting letter, written to a new owner of the London punt gun by its previous user, reads as follows:

Instructions for loading punt gun cartridges

'I am packing off the loading doings today, and hope they arrive safely. You asked for instructions for same but you will know more about it than I do anyway.

The method I used was to cut my papers with a bevel at one end, this is to allow for the slight cone shape in the breech. The size of the paper depends upon the thickness and you will be able to get better papers than I could in those days. Cut as many as you want, coat with paste and leave them for 20 minutes or so, take the iron tube and roll the paper on, and draw out the tube. Allow to harden. Cut the base end as pattern and be careful to cut *just* far enough, the thing being a neat and watertight joint at the base of the cartridge (its surprising how wet they get!)

Push the iron head into the paper, support on wooden roller from the front end, and bend the cut points over, then screw on the rimmed base.

When wadding put a piece of tissue paper in on the wooden roller first, to stop the powder coming out on the spare cartridges. There are eight spare inside parts.

The best results were obtained with 1lb of shot and the same bulk of powder and if you measure this in the small tin, you will see what's what. I used as much wadding (and a card) as I could fit in. (I think 2 felt wads). Put the sizer and the split tube on the case before you start loading, or when you bump the powder and wads the tube will swell, and wax the tube first. The sizer will be about ¹⁄₃₂" open at the split.

Put the 'blank' in last, and unscrew the base while you do it. It fits *below* the surface of the base or should do so.

Make sure there is nothing up the spout, pop the cartridge in the breech with the pin at ½ cock, it has to be anyway to open the breech. Cock the thing and pull on button 'B' and the best of Luck. The important things are: make sure you breeching ropes are tight as poss before you fire, or they will break as easy as a grocer snaps a piece of string, and if that doesn't happen the gun will disappear over the bow of the punt. (I have had the last happen to me, but not the first).

As soon as poss after firing wash the cartridge base and unscrew same, or it will stick tight within half an hour and needs a vice to unscrew it. After firing it is quite easy with the hands.

A really important point is this: if you have got the cartridge stuck in the breech remove the firing pin, take the corkscrew and unload the cartridge from the front end, reverse the ramrod and push the lot out. There is nothing left to explode except the blank and you can hit that from the front end anyway. I've only had to do this once and that was a very rough day, I took a sea up the spout, and hadn't time to stop to remove the cartridge right away, in fact I was considering pitching the whole thing overboard I remember. I have a box of 300 blanks at home and will send them along.'

A description of the London punt gun in the Holland and Holland collection:

The Celebrated 'LONDON' Punt gun, by Holland and Holland, Serial No. 6994, 7' 6" barrel, 1⅜" bore, fitted with trunnions. Lever operated breech-opening, with breech block. Made in 1881. With the gun in a wooden case, probably original, and a set of accessories and components which include a number of card and felt wads, detachable cartridge bases, cleaning rod and fittings, and a quantity of .32 revolver blanks, used for detonating the cartridges.

who signed himself 'Morfe', who reported his results in January 1881. He used a breech loader of 1¾" bore with a 9' barrel and weighing 140lb, and produced the following results on a target six feet square at 80yds.

Powder ozs	Shot ozs	Shot size	Total No.	Total No. on Target	Percentage
4	20	AA	800	145	18
4	22	AA	800	205	25
4½	22	AA	880	205	23
4½	22	SSG	330	57	17
5	24	AA	960	178	18
5	24	SSG	360	70	19
5	24	BB	1680	137	8
5	24	BB	1680	251	14
6	32	AAA	1120	182	16

From these results it would appear that the patterns were somewhat unreliable, but 'Morfe' added that he considered a 6-foot square target too small, suggesting that a 12-foot square target would not be 'a bit too large'.

In February 1881, a correspondent signing himself 'S. S. G.' wrote of his own punt gun trial. He had used a 1⅜ inch breech-loader with a 7-foot cylinder barrel, total weight 63lb, and shot with 15ozs B-shot (86 to the ounce, total 1290) and an equal measure of powder (weight unspecified). Shooting at 80 yds at a 4-foot square target, six shots rendered an average of 211

An early shooter in 1822 sends out a signal of distress.

Testing a punt gun at Holland's Shooting Grounds in about 1910.

striking the target, or approximately 16 per cent. Unfortunately the details of the six shots are not published, and therefore the consistency of the pattern is not known.

Much discussion ensued concerning the size of target which should be used, some advocating square targets, suggestions varying from four feet square to twelve feet square and over. Some suggested a lateral target two feet high and eight to ten feet wide, being more representative of a raft of water-fowl. The problem of lateral dispersal of the pattern exercised several minds at this time, and some punt guns were actually made with an oval bore gradually widening to some eight inches, while narrowing slightly in depth. However any movement in the water when firing caused the shot to pass over or under the fowl, depending on the movement of the punt. In any case the patterns were highly erratic, and the idea was soon scrapped.

What was the attraction of this strange sport? For one view let us quote again from *The Fowler in Ireland*, where Sir Ralph writes,

'Though a wildfowl shooter's existence is often tinged with melancholy, by reason of the broad expanse of waste and shipless water whereon his favourite sport is pursued, still, should game-shooting become monotonous, and impair the energy with which it was wont to be followed, I would say, let such a man hie him to the coast, with its myriads of wary wild birds. There he will be greeted with the scream of the Curlew, the call of the Duck, the clang of the Wild-goose, the trumpet of the Swan, and the mocking laugh of the Great Northern Diver. There his utmost ingenuity will be taxed. Cunning must needs meet cunning, watchfulness, watching; or the bag will be light. The look at the surroundings, what a change! The tides, the sea, wind and weather, all affect him and his sport; all will interest him as they cheer or mar his hopes of success. What a scene is this compared to the never-varying turnip-field, the leafless, dripping wood!'

Not everyone was as successful at punt gunning as Sir Ralph. Malcolm Lyell recalls how the Maharajah of Kolhapur when visiting London for the coronation of Edward VII acquired a Holland punt gun which he was anxious to try out on the lake near his palace. It was mounted in a boat, and, with a *shikari* cowering somewhat nervously behind the loaded gun, pushed gently out to the middle of the water where a large number of duck sat calmly awaiting their fate. The Maharajah gave a signal at what he judged to be the critical moment, and the *shikari* pulled the lanyard. There was an almighty explosion, and boat, gun and *shikari* (who could not swim) sank slowly to the bottom of the lake. The *shikari* was rescued immediately, the gun a few days later. Malcolm Lyell heard this story some sixty years later when he came across the gun lying in the Durbar Hall of the new Palace at Kolhapur unused since that fateful day.

An earlier enthusiast, who was perhaps more successful, was the King of Portugal, and the specification book for his punt guns still remains on the shelves of Holland's archive room.

The entry in the record book for the King of Portugal's Punt Gun.

⚜ 14 ⚜

'No Harm in a Pair of New Guns Each Season'

The Anatomy of Elegance

It has been said that every sportsman who seeks the utmost enjoyment from the possession and use of a gun should learn to recognise elegance. One might add that every craftsman working on a 'best' gun will have elegance, or good design, or fitness for purpose in his mind, too.

To deal first with the most superficial aspect of elegance – the engraving of the metal – the decorated gun seems to be a product of the Renaissance. Pattern books for ornaments on butt plates and barrels were readily available from the 16th century. Elaborate patterns, mounts of gilt and engraved bronze were produced by the craftsmen of the day. Staghorn and ivory was inlaid into wooden stocks. Steelwork was chiselled. Exotic woods were carved. The work of these men has now found its way to museums like the Victoria and Albert; the scholars ascribe guns to artists – in the same way that paintings are so ascribed – with exotic names like the Master of the Animal Headed Scroll, a celebrated stock-maker of the 17th century whose real name is unknown.

By the 18th century, such decoration, particularly in France, had reached the state of high art; indeed at a Versailles factory, the boss Boutet styled himself Directeur Artiste and produced some of his finest work for Napoleon.

The London makers, helped perhaps by the pioneer work of French and other continental engravers, followed the fashion in ensuring that their guns were engraved to the higest degree, and this tradition of excellence in engraving has continued to the present day. The fact is that the quality of engraving over the past 25 years has been higher than it has ever been, surpassing the earlier Royal and 'de luxe' patterns which were usually to a standard design.

A writer in the *New York Herald Tribune*, commenting on the visit to New York of Messrs. Lyell and Clarke in 1966 had this to say:

'. . . Most American sportsmen shooters, collectors and gun nuts generally are aware that one does not attempt to describe fine firearms with words. Rather, one picks a piece up and feels its delicate balance, snuggles it to his shoulder and sights along the barrels, swinging the gun at an imaginary moving target, skyward if at waterfowl or upland birds, parallel with the horizon if the target is running.

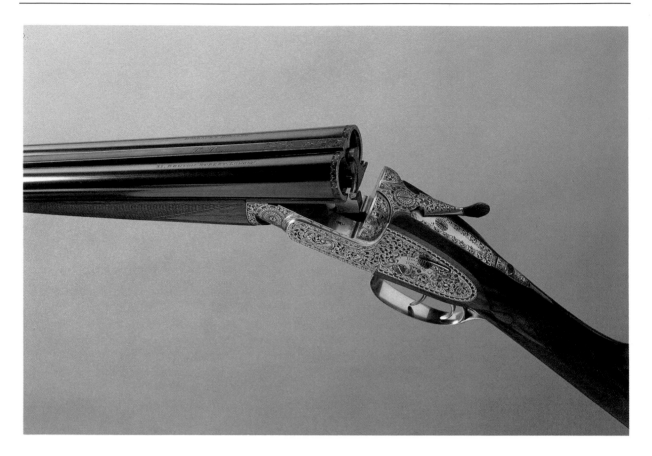

If a shotgun, he breaks it and peers down the gleaming corridors of the barrels. He inspects the engraving, picking out a figure of Diana and her drawn bow, a leaping stag, a sweep-tailed pheasant, a hustling grouse. He shakes his head and invariably he asks the expert:

A 12-bore Holland & Holland 'Royal' shotgun with Royal scroll engraving.

"How long did it take to do this work?"

The expert smiles and thinks for a moment and then gives him his answer, not in days, weeks or months, but in total hours because that is the way these artists work – a few hours now, a few hour later, and the hours can add up to three weeks or two months.

As Malcolm Lyell says of a shotgun whose 23-carat gold inlaid engraving he designed for the Ruler of Qatar, a British-protected sheikdom on the Persian Gulf claimed by Saudi Arabia, "Who knows, really? One works now, one works again – anything to avoid becoming bored with the design or weary of the task. The design takes form, the figures emerge and suddenly it is done. At times it is almost a shock to know the job is finished".'

This passion for elegance is one which Lyell possesses to a marked degree. He describes how he put this to the development of special sets of guns and rifles. 'The person who made such an impression on me was Louis Vranken, during my first visit to the Fabrique Nationale in Liege in 1964. They had 125 engravers at that time. But there were two special engravers, separated from the rest in cubicles, called Louis Vranken and Watrin. They showed me photographs of work they had done – designs of their own creation and carried out by them. Some were on F.N. Over & Under Browning guns, others on pistols, or even on bayonets. I arranged for Vranken to embellish the action and barrels of a new 12 bore gun which we had made for stock. I very much left it to him to use his imagination, but I did say that I would like Diana, the Goddess of Hunting to be included. The gun was deeply engraved and inlaid in gold and silver. We exhibited it at the Game Fair at Chatsworth in 1966. Gough Thomas, probably the greatest gun writer in the world, said in *The Shooting Times*: "This gun must be one of the finest and most elaborately decorated guns ever produced in modern times . . . Gold is used freely for decoration; but the final effect, though rich, is without the glittery appearance suggested by the photograph."

'It was this gun which was the forerunner of our "products of excellence", although the idea for a set of five guns occurred to me just before Christmas 1965. Actually what started me thinking about this was when I went round to wish the two Wilkes brothers in Beak Street a happy Christmas. In the course of our conversation they said that their father and uncle had talked about a set of guns in different bores. They said they would love to see something like this put into effect. And this was the start of the 1968 Set of Five.

'It should be made quite clear that whilst many of these guns may have been highly ornamented, they are all technically perfect functioning guns which can give as many years service provided they are cared for, as any standard Holland & Holland "Royal". Many of them are in regular use – but others

One of the 1983 Wildfowler and Wader guns shown resting across the cleaning drawer especially fitted to take the superb set of tools. The original designs for engravings were mounted in leather and included with the set.

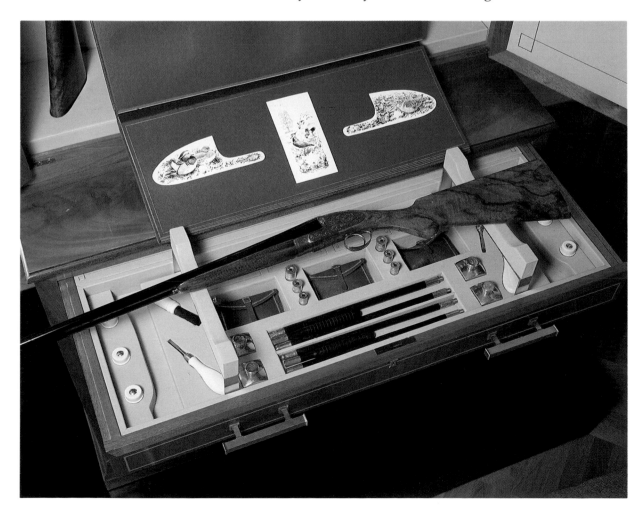

have never been shot since they were bought and regarded by their owners as collectors pieces. Actually they are all collectors pieces. The *Daily Telegraph* described the Broadlands set as "instant antiques".'

The first Set of Five was designed to meet the challenge of making a set of five guns, each in of a different bore, to identical stock measurements. This was successfully achieved and a purchaser came forward at the reception at which the guns were displayed for the first time. In the same way, all subsequent sets of guns have been offered for sale only after completion. When a set has been made to commemorate a particular event, part of the proceeds has always been donated to a suitable charity or shooting or conservation organisation.

Commemorative Guns

1968

Set of Five

In the past, matched sets of five, and even more, guns have been made for one person, but always in the same bore size. They were to be found in the gun rooms of the great European nobility and in the armouries of the Indian Princes.

It is almost certain that no matched sets of guns have been made in different bores, and that the 1968 Set of Five Holland & Holland guns is the first of its kind in the history of gunmaking. Each gun was of a popular bore size from 12 gauge down to .410. The set took nearly three years to make from when the idea was conceived.

In the summer of 1966, Mr Earle K. Angstadt Jr., President of Abercombie & Fitch, heard about these guns when he was in London, and immediately asked whether this first set could be reserved for his company. Their manufacture after that was a joint project of Abercombie & Fitch and Holland & Holland.

The making of these guns presented many problems, especially as they had to be perfectly graduated down in the outside form of the actions, trigger guards, and levers and yet still have identically the same stock measurements. The selection of matching stock blanks of beautiful figure was not easy, for walnut of the quality used for these guns is extremely scarce.

It was decided that this unique set of guns must be fitted in an equally rare gun cabinet, and Mr Algernon Asprey, the Managing Director of Asprey's of London, was asked to assist in the designing and making of this cabinet, made by one of the finest cabinet makers in Britain.

1970

The Set of Five

In 1966 another set of five guns was also started which were to be a pair of 12, a pair of 20 and a single 28 bore.

This new set, known as the 1970 Set of Five, was particularly remarkable because of the almost perfect match of the walnut stocks, the magnificient engraving, and the fact that they were the first guns of the new Holland & Holland numbers of the 40,000 series.

The walnut log from which these stocks were cut was specially selected by one of the greatest experts in walnut, Monsieur Jean Teyssier of Brive, who had been asked by

One of the set of Twenty Five Rifles celebrating the Silver Jubilee of Queen Elizabeth II.

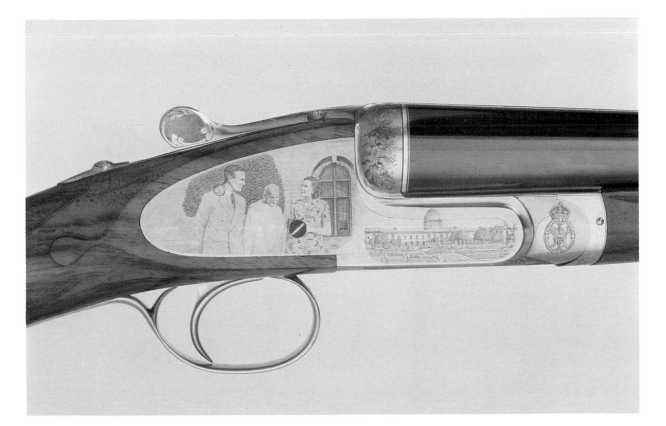

Lord and Lady Mountbatten with Mahatma Gandhi engraved on one of two guns of the Broadlands set.

Holland & Holland to try to find the most perfectly matched stocks that he had ever seen. It was from a walnut tree cut in a valley in north-west Iran that Monsieur Teyssier managed to obtain these stocks, which were of a pale colour with the most unusual rippling figure of fine black lines accompanied by what is known as 'fiddle back'. The wood was so perfectly matched that the stocks could be arranged side by side so as to match one with the next.

The other remarkable feature was the engraving of these guns. This work was carried out by perhaps the finest creative gun engraver in England – Mr Kenneth Hunt – who was asked to engrave the locks and actions of these guns with scenes selected from pictures by the great British wildlife artist, Archibald Thorburn, who died in 1935. Anyone familiar with the work of Thorburn would easily recognise the engraving of the 12 and 20 bores, which is typical of the style of his pictures. The 28 bore, which had scenes of Bob White Quail and Mourning Doves engraved on the lock plates, was done in the same style, although there are no known pictures by Thorburn of these two species.

The Brazilian rosewood cabinet was specially made by one of England's finest cabinet makers, to a design by Mr Algernon Asprey in whose workshops in Bond Street the elaborate interior leather work and fittings were prepared. Lyell's expressed aim was to show that things of great individuality and superb workmanship could still be made in Britain.

1977

The Jubilee Sets

In 1971 Holland & Holland finished a remarkable 12 bore gun which was entitled 'The Art of the Engraver and Embellisher',

Two patterns of Gun Cabinets by Lang.

LEFT: *The Broadlands Set of Four Guns 1984.*

which was superbly engraved and inlaid with many different precious and semi-precious metals portraying British Mammals, Birds and Fishes. Its destination was to be the British Fortnight in San Francisco.

In the year of Her Majesty The Queen's Silver Jubilee 1977, Holland & Holland presented another superb set of guns. This set consisted of a pair of 12 and a pair of 20 bore guns, engraved on the lock plates and actions with scenes of the Queen during her reign. Except for one informal scene of the Queen and the Duke of Edinburgh in Scotland, all the engravings portrayed the Queen at formal occasions during the previous twenty-five years, beginning with the left lock of the No. 1 gun showing the scene in Westminster Abbey after the crowning. Around these scenes were engraved the floral emblems of Britain, and on the trigger guards are shields with the crosses of St. George, St. Andrew, and St. Patrick, and the Welsh Dragon.

This unique set of guns was fitted in a cabinet designed by Algernon Asprey Ltd. and made by Gordon Russell Ltd. from specially selected Macassar Ebony – almost certainly the first gun cabinet to have been made in this wood. The upper part of the cabinet was inlaid with silver of the four floral emblems of the United Kingdom – hall marked in London with the Jubilee mark.

In addition to this set of guns Holland & Holland made a set of twenty-five Silver Jubilee magazine rifles – one for each of the Queen's reign. There were five rifles in each of the calibres 7mm Remington Magnum, .300 Winchester Magnum, .308 Winchester, .375 Holland & Holland Magnum and .458 Winchester Magnum.

These rifles were inlaid in silver on the magazine cover plates with the official Silver Jubilee emblem, and with the Set Number of the rifle. Between the spear fore-sight and back-sight ramps the barrels were inlaid in silver with the name and address of Holland & Holland.

1983
The Wildfowl and Wader Set

This set of wildfowl and wader guns commemorate the founding in 1908 of the Wildfowlers' Association of Great Britain and Ireland, familiarly known as WAGBI, the purpose being to celebrate the 75th Anniversary of the founding of the Association, and to apply some of the proceeds of the sale of the guns to the Association.

From the inception of the idea it was decided that this set of guns would be engraved with as many scenes as possible of the different species of geese, ducks and waders of the world. It was also decided that a prominent British wildlife artist should be invited to prepare the drawings for the engraving. Rodger McPhail accepted the commission, and Ken Preater, Supervisor of the Holland & Holland engraving school, accepted the challenge of interpreting the McPhail drawings on metal. The original drawings also included plants, small mammals, fish and reptiles of the shores, lakes, moorlands and fields inhabited by wildfowl. These original drawings were contained in a folio in a drawer in the cabinet.

1984

The Broadlands Set

A set of four guns were started in 1980 and in 1983 it was thought it would be appropriate for this set to commemorate the 1984 Game Fair at Broadlands, the home of Lord Mountbatten. His grandson, Lord Romsey, to whom the house and property were left on Lord Mountbatten's death, agreed to the proposal, but felt that as far as it was possible the theme should illustrate the history of Broadlands, with special emphasis on his grandmother, Lady Mountbatten, who inherited the property through her father.

As much as possible of the history of the house and its distinguished owners was portrayed in the engraving of the eight lock plates and four actions. It was decided to engrave the first gun with three scenes of episodes in Lord Mountbatten's life up to the end of the Second World War, the second gun with scenes showing Lord and Lady Mountbatten during the period when they were Viceroy and Vicereine of India in

Elegance is carried into every aspect. Complete with tools in a velvet-lined oak and leather case, this rifle was supplied in 1884 to HH The Nizam of Hyderabad.

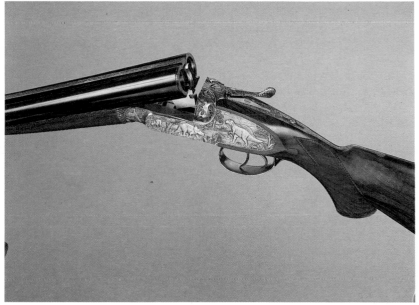

ABOVE RIGHT: *Sculptured engraving. The pre-historic scene of the Saurian 4-bore.*

1947. The number three and four guns portrayed scenes of the family and the house up to Christmas 1983 with an engraving of Lord and Lady Romsey and their two children.

The engravings on other parts of each gun were linked to the period of the principal gun engraving scenes so far as was possible – for example, the knuckles of the number one gun were engraved with two wartime decorations of Lord Mountbatten, one British and the other American, whilst the number two gun had two orders connected with India. In the same way the floral engravings were all taken from photographs of shrubs and plants named after members of the family.

The very high standard of engraving – particularly the portraiture, was achieved by what is now referred to as 'dot' engraving – a painstaking process requiring great concentration on the part of the engraver. It was the first time that this technique was used in Britain on the steelwork of guns. Engraving from photographs presents considerable difficulties and some scenes had to be adapted to fit the shapes of the actions and locks.

The cabinet was designed in the style of the Victorian mahogany book case in the Palmerston room at Broadlands.

1985 and 1988
The Saurian and Herculean guns

In the latter part of the 19th century a small number of breechloading large bore rifles and guns were made by British gunmakers. Eight and four-bore guns were comparatively common and favoured by the professional market gunners who supplied wildfowl for the table. Most of these guns were hammered but some hammerless examples are known. The rifles are much rarer because they were quickly superceded by the high velocity small calibre "Express" rifle for big game shooting.

Holland & Holland had made a very small number of 4-bore hammer guns and rifles and even one 4-bore hammerless ejector double barrel rifle which was supplied to one of the Indian princes in 1924. In 1969 it was decided that Holland & Holland would make another double barrel 4-bore hammerless ejector. This was to be a smooth bore shot gun and when the order was placed in the factory Mr. Geoffrey Brooks, production director, thought it safer to make two "in case the first went wrong". In point of fact both "went right".

The first, the Saurian Gun, was sculpted and engraved with scenes of dinosaurs and other creatures of the period – and some yet older – together with the vegitation then existing. The Saurian gun represents a new peak in the renaissance of British gun engraving which began about 20 years ago and, with the massive size of the action and barrels, it is a fitting canvas to portray some of the largest animals which have ever walked the earth, and which ruled it for almost 140 million years.

It was thought appropriate to fit the gun in a lizard skin case, and to present it in a chest with a collection of fossil relics including the egg and a coprolite of a dinosaur. In addition the chest contained a lizard skin cartridge magazine with one hundred 4-bore cartridges from the last loading in the Eley-Kynoch factory.

It was decided to engrave the second gun with the awesome Labours of Hercules. The scenes on the action, lock plates and furniture have been sculpted and engraved from seven of the Twelve Labours. The composition of the embellishment is without parallel – and to portray such mythological scenes the engraver must have a deep feeling for the subject which, as the accompanying illustrations show, has been achieved to a masterly degree. The Herculean gun was also complimented by one hundred 4-bore cartridges.

1987
The set of four British Field Sports Guns

In June 1984 it was decided that a set of four Holland & Holland "Royal" shotguns would be made engraved with scenes portraying typical field sports of the British Isles. The manufac-

The Herculean 4-bore finished in 1988, sculpted with the Labours of Hercules. Inset: foresight – the Hercules beetle.

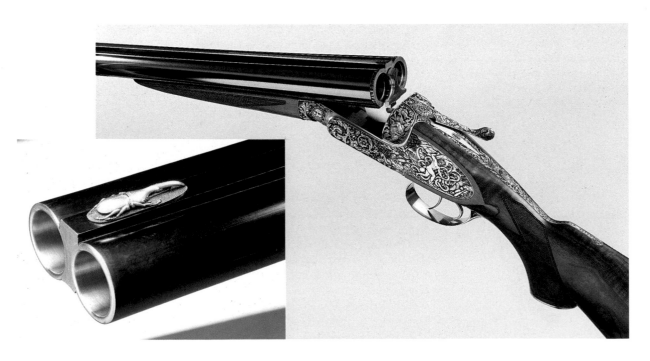

ture of these guns in the Holland & Holland factory in London commenced the following month. They were the seventh set of special guns made by the Company during the past twenty years.

The famous British wildlife artist, Rodger McPhail, was commissioned to draw the scenes for the engraving of the lock plates and the underside of the actions. The original drawings are bound in a folder contained in the cabinet. The other parts of the actions and the furniture of each gun have been engraved with vignettes complimentary to the main scenes, and are taken from paintings and sketches in Rodger McPhail's book, *Open Season – An artist's sporting year*, published in 1986. The engraving has been carried out by Ken Preater, supervisor of the Holland & Holland engraving school. The guns have been fitted in a cabinet designed and constructed by Vince Rickards who made the cabinet for the 1984 Broadlands set of guns.

1985
The Classical Series

In 1985 it was decided to build a series of Holland & Holland guns which, because of their embellishment, would be known as The Classical Series.

The first gun of this series has become known as the Fourten Rococo Gun, which has been sculpted rather than engraved and the background treated in the manner of some presentation firearms made in Europe, particularly Germany, during the middle part of the 18th century. Gold was deposited using a special technique rather than inlaid.

The gun has been sculpted with mythological Grecian scenes surrounded by rococo style relief engraving. The composition of the embellishment and the technical quality of the engraving of this gun has probably never been surpassed during the whole history of gun engraving.

The Four-ten Rococo gun. Detail of heel plate – Nessus the Centaur carrying off Deianeira – and right lock – Perseus and Andromeda.

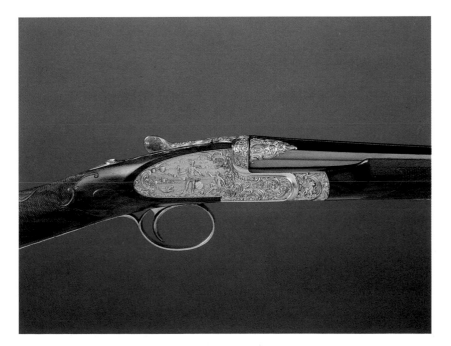

1987

The African Hunter Series

In 1987 Holland & Holland began a series of rifles in .500/.465 calibre which commemorate the greatest of the African hunters. In selecting names from the long list of candidates, only those were picked whose contribution could be judged by merits other than the mere size of their game books. Whilst there were many great hunters, only a few could claim to have been explorers and pioneers who played a real role in the 'discovery' of Africa.

The first rifle, serial number 35550, commemorates Sir Samuel Baker, 1821-1893, a man who has been described as 'the perfect Victorian hero'. Of all the hunters, Baker was probably the most widely experienced, having hunted in every continent. As a firearms enthusiast he hunted through the crucial period of change from muzzle-loading to modern breech-loading guns and 'Express' rifles. Perhaps the most famous rifle ever fired in Africa was his "Baby", a single muzzle-loading rifle by Holland which fired a half-pound explosive shell and which the Arabs called 'child of a cannon'!

Baker was a gifted naturalist who achieved the acclaim of the Royal Geographical Society and, as Governor General of the Nile Basin, did much to suppress the slave trade there before handing over to General Gordon. It is a tribute to his tenacity that he survived to die in his home in England, at the age of 72.

Number two in the series is the 'Selous' rifle. Unlike Baker, who came to hunting as a pastime, Frederick Courtenay Selous, 1851-1916, was fired with the ambition for adventure at an early age. He landed in Africa in 1871 and set out to hunt commercially with a zeal which would make up for his poor equipment and lack of resources; he survived the ravages of illness, exhaustion and animals by strength of spirit alone.

Besides his hair-raising encounters with elephant, Selous is remembered for his exploratory work, penetrating deep into unknown territory. In this way he played a significant role in securing the territory of Rhodesia for the British Crown by opening up the country to the British South Africa Company.

Selous hunted trophies in many parts of the world and such was his international fame that it was to him that Roosevelt would come to organise his African hunting trips. When killed in action in German East Africa fighting for the Allies his death was mourned by his enemy commander and even by the Kaiser himself.

The third rifle commemorates W. D. M. Bell, 1880-1951, and number four will commemorate R. G. G. Cumming. 1820-1866. Further rifles in the series will remember Harris, Baldwin, Neumann, Powell-Cotton, and Hunter.

It is clear that the expansion of Holland & Holland's business into the appurtenances of guns, as well as guns themselves, had gone pretty far by 1990. The magnificent cabinets made by the craftsmen for some of the commemorative sets is witness of that. But it has to be admitted that the firm has not yet set up a complete furnishing department for the client's gun room which, as a writer in 1905 explained, 'is generally one of the snuggest, even if not the most luxurious, in the mansion . . .

The Baker gun. Detail of the first African Hunter Rifle. Portrait of Sir Samuel Baker.

A scene from the life of Frederick Courtney Selows.

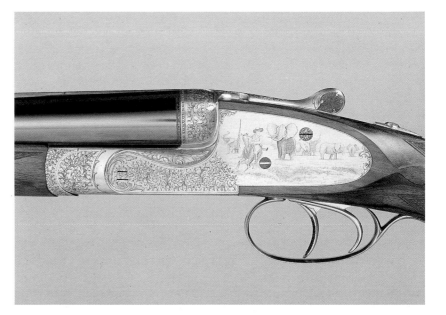

The set of four British Field Sports guns. Detail from the Deer Stalking gun (No. 3) and the Game Shooting and Wildfowling gun (No. 1).

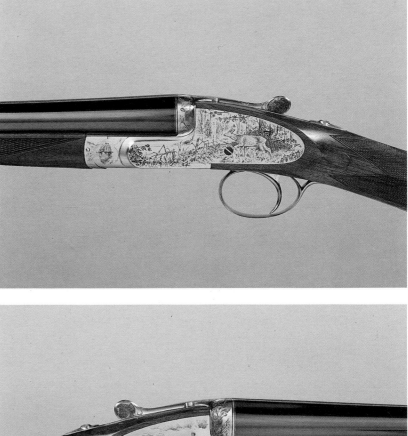

The gun room is often the smoking room of an evening . . . and to the same room, after breakfast, on a hopeless day, tend the steps of the rain-bound sportsman. If properly fitted with battery, and above all, books, there is much not only to interest but to instruct . . . If the volume you take down from the shelf should be unattractive, you subside into dreamland, to awaken refreshed.'

The reader who has come thus far may now subside into slumber, submerged in The Great Gun Room of his dreams, overflowing on all sides with Holland & Holland guns and rifles.

Holland & Holland Sesquicentennial set of 15 Hammer Guns.

Appendices

Appendix I

A curious use for punt guns

A curious use for punt guns has been found in the Holland family archives. It concerns one William Marshall (the Marshalls were Hollands by marriage) who persuaded Harris Holland sometime in the middle of the 19th century to aid him in an exotic enterprise in the Straits of Malacca. Henry Holland's account of this is as follows:

William Marshall was apprenticed to some trade in London but being of a roving disposition he ran away and went to sea. I did not know anything of his movements until a time some years after. He spent a good deal of his time I know on the coast of Asia Minor and did business in Smyrna. There he met a man named Lovey, and together they worked up a diving business. Eventually they bought the 'Wizard' a schooner of about 90 tons. Various successes and failures I believe followed but taking it on the whole they were fairly successful. The great coup however was the searching for a sunken ship in the Straits of Malacca. It appears that a Spanish ship, known to be freighted with gold in bullion and coin had been sunk there, I believe very many years before, and various efforts had been made to find her but in consequence of the amount of silting up with sand that goes on in that locality she had not been found. Marshall came over here to fit out, get new diving dress etc. He came to Uncle Harris to get some sort of weapon which would be useful against Chinese pirates; the place was infested with these. Uncle Harris supplied him with six swivel duck guns; these were about 8 or 9 feet long and 1½" bore, carrying about 1¼lbs of big slugs and a large charge of powder. These fired at say from 100 to 200 yards, gave a spread of shot of some 12 or 15 feet and would be likely to damage and sink the very light craft used by the pirates. I do not know the name of the people who fitted out the diving dress. I have forgotten it. Eventually Marshall arrived in the Straits with the 'Wizard' schooner and began dragging for the sunken ship. If you look at the map you will see the enormous area he would have to drag. I believe he got some information from the natives who gave him some idea of the probable locality of the sunken ship. This must be some 70 years ago and as well known in those days all these Eastern seas were very dangerous in conse-quence of the great number of pirates who came out in quite large junks and were pretty desperate men. Now for ordinary ships these were looked upon as dangerous but how much more so to a small schooner which had to hang about in the same locality month after month. Marshall was attacked many times but usually was able to beat off the pirates' junks in consequence of the effect of those slugs fired from the duck guns, but on one occasion the pirates succeeded in boarding the schooner and were only beaten off after some loss sustained by the schooner's crew. I might here mention that most of the expert divers were either Greeks or Turks. I remember Marshall saying that the Greeks were the best men at the job as they appeared to be able to stay under water longer than any other men Mr Lovey came across. I believe they used to carry on the search by towing a drag with grappling irons between two boats going systematically over the ground. Eventually they came across a sunken ship which was practically covered with this silted sand and after an immense amount of work they got into the body of the ship which proved to be the prize they were seeking and eventually into the treasure house, and found the long looked for treasure. It was packed up in small boxes about 10 or 12 inches square. I remember seeing one of those boxes. I am not sure but I believe most of the gold was in bars but there was also I think a large quantity of Spanish doubloons or some such gold coins. How much the treasure was worth I do not know but they eventually got it all up and took it to some Bank in Singapore and it was from there sent to London under I think a guard of soldiers but this may have been when taken to the Singapore Bank. Marshall told me that there was a long article about this extraordinary affair in *The Times* (2 or 3 columns) and it is just possible by searching the columns of *The Times* or writing to the Editor this might be found. Of course you understand I only remember, and that not very clearly what Marshall told me. The sad part of it was this. The agreement between Lovey and Marshall was that they should share and share alike, but there was no proper partnership deed. Sailors are very often bad business men. Lovey had in the meantime got into financial trouble and his creditors laid in a shop or attachment upon whatever monies there might be due to Lovey's estate in connection with the salvage because it was Lovey's ship and Marshall could not prove the partnership. Of course you are aware that when insurance has been paid upon a sunken ship or its cargo and these are salvaged afterwards a certain proportion of the salvage results has to be paid to the underwriters. However I believe that Marshall did get some money somehow but he never got anything like what he should have done had there been a proper deed of partnership. I think Marshall spent over two years in his seafaring search – carried out very often under the greatest dangers and difficulties.

Appendix II

Gun numbers

Paradox Guns

No.	Year
15036	1895
347	1895
558	1900
655	1903
750	1905
825	1906
860	1907
900	1911
950	1914
960	1919
970	1922
980	1930

Best Guns

No.	Year
22000	1899
22500	1900
23000	1902
23500	1903
25000	1906
25500	1907
25599	1910
27000	1910
250	1911
500	1912
750	1913
999	1914
29000	1914
100	1915
200	1919
300	1920
400	1920
499	1921
30500	1921
600	1922
700	1922
800	1924
900	1925
999	1926
31500	1926
600	1927
700	1927
800	1928
900	1929
999	1929
32500	1929
600	1930
700	1930
800	1931
900	1932
999	1934
33000	1934

Best Guns

No.	Year
33000	1934
100	1935
200	1936
300	1937
400	1937
500	1939
600	1946
700	1948
800	1950
900	1952
33999	1954
36251	1954
300	1956
400	1958
500	1959
600	1962
700	1964
800	1965
900	1967
900	1970
40006	1970
100	1972
200	1974
300	1978
400	1978
500	1979

Plain Guns

No.	Year
26200	1907
300	1908
400	1909
500	1909
600	1910
700	1911
800	1912
900	1913
999	1913
28600	1913
700	1914
800	1914
900	1915
999	1915
29500	1915
600	1915
700	1916
800	1919
900	1919
30000	1919
100	1920
200	1922
300	1924
30334	1925
31100	1925
31200	1926
300	1928
399	1929
32200	1929
300	1931
400	1933
499	1935
34000	1935
100	1936
200	1937
300	1939
400	1949
500	1953
600	1956
700	1961
800	1975

Double Rifles

.450 & .465		.375		.240 & Small bores	
28200	1910	28400	1911	228566	1920
299	1914	499	1920	599	1923
28500	1914	30416	1920	31000	1923
565	1919	499	1925	31041	1926
30335	1921	31050	1925	31400	1926
30415	1921	099	1927	450	1931
31042	1925	32100	1927	499	1955
31049	1925	32199	1933		
32000	1927				
32099	1941				

Single Rifles

No.	Year
28000	1910
100	1911
199	1913
28300	1913
399	1919

New series from 1.

All Bores

No.	Year
35000	1933
100	1939
200	1950
250	1953
300	1956
350	1958
400	1963
450	1968
500	1974

Under & Over Guns

No.	Year
3600	1950
010	1952
020	1954
036	1967

Appendix III

Records in possession of Holland & Holland relating to weapons made prior to 1893

The records still in existence begin with serial No. 541, and the first date to be found is March 1856 at serial No. 565. The next date to be found is October 1856 at serial No. 580. As there are seven months between the dates of production of the twenty-five weapons between 565 and 580, it may be reasonable to assume that a similar interval might have elapsed between 541 and 565, or twenty-four weapons. It may therefore be assumed that the existing records begin around the latter end of 1855.

The details given at this early period are in most cases extremely brief, and in the remainder they have not been entered. A typical entry might read: 'New double breech-loader 12-bore,' or just 'New breech-loader.' As time went by gradually more detail was entered, but it was not until the 1880s that details such as the length of barrels were to be found, and only by the late 1890s were entered anything approaching full details.

The records begin with weapons by H. Holland, and it will be seen from the list of weapons in the Holland and Holland collection that the early H. Holland guns bear the address '9 King Street, Holborn, London'. In 1866 the company moved to 98 New Bond Street, Mayfair (where it remained until 1960), and in 1876 the company became Holland & Holland.

A strict numerical sequence was adopted until the serial 8999 was reached, in 1887. We have no existing records for serial numbers from 9000 to 10849, both inclusive. An examination of other records in the company leads us to believe that the entire series from 9000 to 9999 was not used, though there may be weapons bearing serial numbers between 10000 and 10849.

The normal series for guns and rifles continued from 10849 to 11000. There were 500 weapons between 11000 and 11499, when the serial again jumped from 11499 to 12000. They took up the entire series from 12000 to 12999, then jumped to 14000, took up the entire series from 14000 to 14999, then jumped to 16000, taking up the entire series from 16000 to 16999. At this point there is a change in the method of dating; hitherto the date of order was recorded, and the weapon could have been completed some time later. From the 16000 series onward the dates shown are those when the weapon was either finished in the factory, or finally shot at the Range.

Rook rifles had their own series, beginning with the series

10850 to 10999, jumping to 13000, and taking up the entire series from 13000 to 13999.

Paradox weapons started their own series from 11500 to 11999, then took up the entire series from 15000 to 15999.

Summary

Normal series Guns & rifles
541 to 8999.
 9000 to 10849 Missing
10850 to 10999 Rook rifles
11000 to 11499 normal series
11500 to 11999 Paradox guns
12000 to 12999 normal series
13000 to 13999 Rook rifles
14000 to 14999 normal series
15000 to 15999 Paradox guns
16000 to 16999 normal series

HOLLAND & HOLLAND
RECORDED DATES
Start with serial No. 541.

565	*March 1856*	
	(First recorded date)	
580	*October 1868*	
584	*February 1857*	
700	*August 1859*	
728–1059	A gap in the	

records

1060		*1864*
1101	*January 1965*	
1352	*January 1868*	
1439	*January 1869*	
1578	*January 1870*	
1769	*January 1871*	
2002	*January 1872*	
2401	*January 1873*	
2759	*January 1874*	
3174	*January 1875*	
3649	*January 1876*	
4179	*January 1877*	
4774	*January 1878*	
5274	*January 1879*	
5819	*January 1880*	
6382	*January 1881*	
7009	*January 1882*	
7473	*January 1883*	
7904	*January 1884*	
8406	*January 1885*	

8809	*January 1886*
8999	*January 1887*
11114	*January 1887*
9000–10849	missing

Rook Rifles
Starting at 10850   *1887*
10850–10999, continued at 13000
(No records 10999–12999)

13106	*January 1889*
13465	*January 1890*
13566	*January 1891*
13674	*January 1892*
13885	*January 1893*

Normal Series
Starting at 11000 (1887) to 11499,
then carried over to 12000

12000	*May 1888*
12268	*January 1890*

Carried over from 12999 to 14000

14045	*January 1891*
14492	*January 1892*
14983	*January 1893*

Carried over from 14999 to 16000
16000 finished *July 1893*

Paradox Series
Started at

11500		*1885*	
		1886	
		1887	
11691		*1888*	
11788			*1889*
11865			*1890*
11948			*1891*
15075			*1892*
16100	finished		*June 1894*
16200	finished		*July 1894*
16300	finished		*December 1894*
16400	finished		*July 1895*
16500	finished		*May 1896*

Appendix IV

Facsimile pages taken from Holland and Holland Experiments book which covers the period 1899–1905

The facsimile pages 203, 205 and 207 are examples of the results of trials carried out between November 1903 and the end of February 1904 on batches of test cartridges. Then Eley, in particular, was experimenting with different components and one batch was loaded with Russian 'Sokota' powder and another with 'Wollersdorf' from Austria. At that period the Experiments book shows that cartridges were tested at least every two or three months, including samples of cartridges loaded by competitors.

At a time when there was intense competition between the leading rifle makers, Holland and Holland were continually experimenting to both maintain and enhance their commanding position in the trade. Pages 7 and 89 record interesting results with .577 bore loadings but from 1900 on there is no doubt that the main preoccupation was with the .375. Pages 234, 242, 246 and 252 give the results of four of many tests that were carried out on this calibre between 1900 and 1905.

180 — *12 bore paradox*

May 12 - 1903

Paradox, 12 bore, Eley case with lining 1·15 from head, obtained standard results with 3 drams (bulk) of the bulk nitros. i.e. 42 grs Schultze, card, 3/8 felt, & card wad, 735 gr bullet, four style of crimping gave :-

O.V. 20 yds 1·008 F.S, Pressures 1"   2½"

998	2·61 tons	2·36 tons
985	2·43	2·46
991	2·11	2·01
995·2	2·21	2·11

and similarly 33 grs E.C. gave

O.V. 20 yds F.S. Pressures 1"   2½"

987	2·58 tons	2·36 tons
947	2·16	2·46
974	2·40	2·01

Imperial Schultze was irregular, This height of lining just takes the charge, so that the powder is not & cannot be compressed.

(signed) F.W.J.

8 Bore   Paradox Proof Barrel 181

Nov 11 - 1903

Bore of Barrel ·890

Dia of Bullet ·890, weight 2¾ ozs plus 20 grs — 1224 grain

Charge	Velo's over 20 yards	Pressures at 1½"	4½"	6"	lead crushers
8 drams N°6	1229	4·65	3·58	2·78	Solid brass case
	1241	4·52	3·55	2·84	
10 drams N°6	1421	5·66	4·50	3·63	
	1374	5·74	4·41	3·30	
45 Grs Rev Cordite	863	1·50	1·50	1·74	
50 " " "	962	2·53	2·46	2·29	
	954	2·21	2·16	2·11	
55 " " "	1088	3·80	3·35	2·75	
	1071	3·00	2·78	2·61	
60 " " "	1154	4·10	3·50	2·84	
	1149	3·95	3·30	2·70	
65 " " "	1201	3·55	3·48	3·14	
	1234	3·88	3·20	3·00	

Note : That the 65 grain pressure are less than the 60 grain at 1½ in, & 4½ inch.

(signed) F.W.J.

186 27 March 1903.   (Mr Jones)

Pressures of 12 bore Paradox cartridges
loaded with "Revolver" Cordite and Conical bullet.
Lining 1" from face of case,
wadding. Card, ³⁄₈ felt, Card, with usual
bullet ·735 grain, case crimped into
cannelure of bullet.   lead   crushers
          pressures at   1"   2½"

	1"	2½"
30 grains	3·17	2·78
32 grs	3·78	3·35
35 grs	4·52	3·85
" grs	4·73	4·05

	unpressed copper at 1"	lead at 2½"
40 grs	6 57	5·2
" "	6·22	5·0
	unpressed copper at 1"	lead 2½"
43 grs	6·92	5·6
" "	7·96	6·0
	copper 1"	lead 2½"
46 grs	10·75	6·9
" "	8·30	6·8

(Signed) F.W.J.

---

27 Nov 1903   Range   187

Trial of Paradox cartridges loaded with
40 grs – 43 grs – 46 grs, Revolver Cordite
loaded in Eley, E.B.T. cases, 1?
lining one inch from face of case,
wadding thick glazed card, ³⁄₈ felt,
& thick glazed card, ordinary
Paradox bullet 735 grs, case ringed
into cannelure of bullet.
Fired out of a pair ordinary Paradox
bls Nº 15646, fitted in experimental action,
weight of bls 4 lb 1oz, length 28",

The cartridges fired with above charges
had no effect on the right barrel,
but the first cartridge loaded with
✳ 43 grs, out of the left barrel, bulged
it slightly at 6½" from breech.
The bls are slightly smaller inside, ·733
(2 points) than usual size, and this
would set up a little higher pressure
also left barrel is slightly smaller on the
outside, but not so much, as to cause a bulge,
✳ this cartridge appeared very strong for
the supposed charge.

---

188   12 Bore Paradox   189

March 30 – 1904   (Eleys)

Trial of 12 Bore 2¾" case Service
Ball cartridges.
loaded with 35 grains Revolver Cordite
·735 grain bullet.

Pressures	1"	2½"	Veloc or 20 yds
Lead {	5·10 tons	4·25 tons	1181 f/s
Crushers {	5·27 "	4·60 "	1182 "
Copper {	5·35 "		1194 "
Crushers {	5·00 "		1205 "
{	5·17 "		1205 "

(Service cartridges for "Rajah Roys" paradox)
May 9th – 1904   (Eleys)
Trial of Nitro Paradox cfc, loaded 35 grains
Revolver cordite. 735 grain bullet 2¾" case
Pressures   1"   2½"   Velocities ov 20 yds

lead crushers.	1"	2½"	Velocities
	5·62	4·63	1226
	4·88	4·05	1227
	5·70	4·57	1245
	5·94	4·69	1271
	5·08	4·41	1224
	5·30	4·10	1251
	5·42 tons	4·41 tons	1241 f/s

---

10 Bore Paradox
Bore of 10 bore Paradox bls. not to be
less than ·805 dia, Choke ?
10 Bore paradox bullets to be ·808 dia

March 16 – 1904   (W.G.W)
Tested Samples of 12 bore, and
16 bore Damp-proof, Nitro paradox
lined cases. and approved of same.
"I am using 25 grains in the 12 bores
and 23 grains in the 16 bores, as these
charges work out to a foot in velocity,
compared with cfc I have been using,
and the lining suit either charge.
The 12 bore are the best we have had,
they make a nice length cartridge,
and if they keep the linings an
even length and flash holes one size,
we shall have no trouble with them,
(Signed) W.G.W.   memo 109.

190. **10 Bore Paradox**

"Eley Bros" 13 Oct 1903
Results obtained with No 6 Black Powder in 10 bore Proof barrel.

	O.V	Pressures 1½" 4"	
7 drms (192 grains)	1337 F.S	5·96 + 4·41	Card ½" felt + card
	1348 "	5·90 + 4·39	Bullet out 0·5

	O.V	1½"	4"	
8 drms (219 grains)	1448 "	6·40	4·98	} lead
	1466 "	6·72	5·30	} crushers
	1466 "	6·92	—	} copper crushers
	...0 lost "	6·57	—	} at 1½" only

card, ⅜" felt, card, bullet out 0·55

We have also made some tests with "Cordite", a canelured case to support wads, and prevent the compression of the charge, appears to be essential, we recommend the canelure at 1½" from face for Chopped Cordite and at 1" for Revolver Cordite.

We prefer Revolver Cordite, on account of the difficulty of igniting Chopped Cordite, and also the large amount of unburnt left by that powder.

(Signed) F.W.J.

---

191. **10 Bore Paradox.**

"Eley Bros" 13th Oct 1903
10 Bore Proof Barrel. Brass Case.

Charge	Vels over 20 yds	Pressures 1½"	Pressures 4"	Wadding	Canelure at.	Bullet projects
Chopped Cordite	F.S.	lead	crushers	card. 1½" felt + card	(cracks on powder)	
45 grains	544	nil	nil	" 1½" "		0·5"
50 "	630	1·00	1·00	" 1½" "		·5
70 "	922	2·11	2·25	" 1¼" "		·5
90 "	1107	3·88	3·28	" 1" "		·4
100 "	1264	4·52	3·90	· ½" ·	1⅝" up	0·5"
110 "	1581	5·92	5·53	" ½" "		·5
120 "	1643	8·18	6·22	" ½" "		·5
Revolver Cordite				card. felt card		
40 grains	1112	4·30	3·55	" 1½" "	⅝"	0·6"
42 "	1164	4·75	3·60	" 1½" "	⅝"	·6
45 "	1231	5·86	4·32	" 1¼" "	¾"	·5
45 "	1184	5·30	3·85	" 1" "	1"	·5
50 "	1338	6·26	4·75	" 1" "	1"	·5
50 "	1278	6·16	4·57	" 1" "	1"	·5
55 "	1416	6·37				

Note: All the Chopped Cordite shots, left considerable amount of unburnt.

---

192. **Paradox**

April 20 - 1904   Range

Trial of 12 bore bullets for Expansion.

No 1. is the ordinary old pattern H.P. bullet 735 grains.

No 2. is the old pattern bullet with a medium large hole, weight about 710 grs

No 3. is the old pattern bullet with an extra large hole, weight about 685 grs

No 4. is the new shape "Nitro" pattern H.P. bullet 735 grain.

Fired 6 - 12 bore Paradox bullets, with Cordite, into fine mould, (which had been through a 3/16" mesh sieve.)

No 1 + 2, are the ordinary new pattern H.P. "Nitro" bullet, both penetrated 2 ft 9 in, and did not expand.

No 3. is the medium size hole, (made new shape) which penetrated 2 ft 3 in, and front opened out

No 4. same as No 3. penetrated 1ft 9in and front opened out very much.

193. continued

No 5. is the extra large hole (bullet made new shape) penetrated 2 ft 2 in and front expanded very well.

No 6. same as No 5 penetrated 1 ft 9in and opened out very much.

These large hole bullets are very incertain in their action, No 4 was a medium large hole one, and if it had hit an animal with hard skin or tough muscle, would probably have only caused a surface wound. The new bullets should do better has they have a little longer and deeper hole, than the old pattern.

(see sample bullets)

(signed) W.G.W

194 *Paradox*

Sept 1st 1904   Range No 132

Shooting of heavy 12 bore No 15734
(Hendersons) weight of gun. 7:15, barrels 4:0
length 28 inch, turn of rifling 1 in 38"
Regulated for 4 drams No6 Powder
735 grain bullet 2¾" case
10 shots at 100 yards, in a group of
4" + 4" (in a strong and gusty wind)
this is the best shooting I ever got at
100 yards when using 4 drams.
also tried the gun with the equivalent
of "Cordite" viz 30 grains, and new shape
bullet, in the 2¾" case, and got a
very fine group at 100 yards; 8 shots all
in 2½" + 2½", 7 were in 2" + 2". The gun
gave a muzzle velocity of 1146 F.S with
30 grains of Cordite, which is 60 ft higher
than obtained with 4 drms & old style rifling
Also tried the right bl of this gun with
ordinary 12 bore charge of Cordite (25 grs)
at 200 yards, and got a group of 6
consecutive shots in 3½" + 5" which
is very good.

203

10 Dec 1903   (Eley's)
Trial of E.C.3 ctg, 35 grains 1 oz No5
12 bore Pegamoid case M.C primer,
turnover normal, Sample ctg. from loading
shop, as loaded for H & H.

Pressures	1"	6"	Velocity
	3·20	1·56	1085
	2·75	1·56	1062
	3·03	1·79	1117
	2·61	1·79	1057
	2·75	1·68	1063
	2·87	1·69	1077

Patterns	109	
12 bore	120	With one exception
No 52310	64	this is a very good
R. Barrel	108	series of patterns,
cylinder	109	due we think to
	111	the "Pegamoid"
	97	case, making
	102	a turnover of less
	116	resistance than
	114	an ordinary case
	108	

(signed) F.W.J

205

18th Dec 1903   Range

Trial of 12/5 Pegamoid cartg,
marked Eley "Lab" loading Dec 1/1903
loaded with 35 grains E.C.3. with thick
glazed card wad, 7/16 felt, thick glazed
wad 1 oz No5 shot, thin card over.
cylinder barrel of test gun.

Pattern	Penetration
78	3.36
96	3.38
110	
106	2.81
70	3.12
85	3.16
90	
91	
106	
91	

The patterns are very irregular, and
patchy, and penetration is a little
irregular, and recoil is slightly sharper
than the ordinary Sch, this charge
of powder is too heavy for the charge
of shot to give good results

(signed) W.G.W

207

Feb 9–1904   Range

Trial of ctg loaded with E.C.3.
powder & 1oz of Shot.
32 grains E.C. No3 Field card,
½" felt, thin card 1oz No6 shot,
thin card over, Badminton case
square turnover.
Cylinder barrel of test gun

pattern	penetration	Velocity
116 x 40 yds,		over
146	2·47	20 yds
158	2·33	
150	2·28	at 1017 f.s
139	2·50	
116 x	2·39	
137		

Shots marked x were good patterns, but
a little more open than the others.
the patterns & penetration are good,
and velocity is good for the charge
taking the time of year,
these ctgs give a very easy recoil.

(Signed) W.G.W.

v.s.   89.

Dec 10 - 1903   Range

·577 bore

80 grains Cordite & 560 grain bullet
        Muzzle Velocity   Energy
average   1590   F.S   3140 Ft-lbs

85 grains Cordite & 560 grain bullet

av   1685   F.S   3527 Ft-lbs

90 grains Cordite & 560 grain bullet

av   1868   F.S   4332 Ft-lbs

The ·577 shot very well with 85 grs
and 90 grs, each bll made less than
a 2" group at 100 yards, with both
charges, as against a 4" group with
black powder out of each barrel, and
the velocities are very regular with
these two charges of Cordite.

·577. Pressures
        Cordite   Bullet
Kg   100 grs & 750 grs   15 tons
Eley   "   "   14 "

proof charge   26 tons

above charge heated to 160°
                    20 tons

7

From September to November 1899
Field Experiments Cordite and Black Powder
577 Bore
Cordite 76 gr 560 gr Nickel coated Solid bullet Wads Jute Wax Jute
        2¾ in Eley Case and loading

Muzzle Velocity	Pressure	Pressure after Exposure to 120° Fah° for 12 Hours	Pressure after the bullet was pushed in ⅛ in
Average 1667	6.99	5.85	7.89

Cordite 80 gr 520 gr lead bullet Hollow point Wads Jute wax jute
        2¾ in Eley Case and loading

| Average 1755 | 7.73 | 6.21 | 8.31 |

Black powder 166 gr 570 gr lead Bullet Hollow point Wads Jute Cloth
        3 in Eley Case and loading

Muzzle Velocity ft Sec		Pressures	
Average 1723		10.37	

234.   ·375 Bore

Mr. Jones.   August 23rd 1902
   ·375/270   Kynochs loading
Shot on August 22nd. Thermometer: Dry 68°
Powder. Cordite. 40 grains.
Bullet. Soft Nose. 270 "

Velocity	Pressure Crushers					
	1"			8"		
	before	after	tons	before	after	tons
2040	·461	·458	14·86	·490	·481	8·20
2050	"	·448	15·90	"	·479	8·80
2052	"	·452	15·08	"	·480	8·50
2078	"	·447	16·10	"	·479	8·80
2065	"	·451	15·30	"	·480	8·50
			15·45			8·56

   "You will see the pressures were quite
3 tons less than the 320 grain bullet, these
are however high for the energy given to
the bullet, This high pressure is no doubt
due to the small space given to the 40 grs charge.
In the 320 grs cartridge the density of loading
is 0·84, as against 0·67 in the ·303, and
0·78 in the ·375/270

---

242.   ·375 bore.

Woolfrey   11th March 1903
          Test of new ·375 bore barrel, in
crusher gauge, with our ordinary ·375
cartridges 40 gr Cordite & 270 gr H.P. bullet
and 320 grain. Soft nose solid.
270 grs. H.P. bullet.
Pressures at 1"   2 5/8 "   8"
     tons   9·51   10·63   4·28

320 grain soft nose solid
Pressures at 1"   2 5/8 "   8"
     tons   12·77   14·12   4·69
These results give at least 3 tons less
pressure in chamber than any previous
pressures taken with cartridges of similar
load & depth of bullet in cases.
   The decrease at 8" is not quite so much
in proportion which shows that bullet
must travel up barrel quicker.
                              W. G. W.

Bore of new barrel ·370 depth of groove ·3½

---

246. ·375 bore   Nov 4th 1903

"Woolfreys" report on ·375 cartridges refered
to on page 245.
   ·375 bore ctg. 270 grain H.P. bullet
seated in case 5/8 length overall 2"·960
(ctgs loaded sometime in 1902) (recd 14/12/03)
"these ctg shot well, and made a
group only 1¼" up & down,"

·375 bore ctg, 270 grain Soft nose
solid bullet, seated 13/32, length overall 3"·1
"these ctgs shoot 3½ in lower than
the H.P. ctg above, and do not
shoot so steady, they make a group
of 3" up & down";

{ W. recommends bullets should be }
{ seated 17/32 " from end of a case }
{ to base of bullet. }

Nov 10-1903. Trial of ·375 sample ctgs
E   40 grains Cordite length 1 13/16, fine
wad, 270 grain S.N. solid bullet, in case 13/32
length overall 3"·09, 10 shots at 100 yds
8 in 2¼ + 2 3/8   2 shots low
Velocity. Muzzle   1919   1396 X
                   1917   1903
                   1933   x bad cartridge?

252

April 1st 1905   (Eley's)

   Trial of ·375 bore Cartridges (Kynochs)
41 grains of "Axite" and 270 grains.
Nickel coated bullet. Military pattern,
from our latest ·375 barrel gave the
following velocities, and pressures,
over 20 yards.
                        Crushers
O.V. 1958 f.s.   ·480 – ·471 = 11·83 tons
     1904 .   "   ·474   11·03 "
     1927 .   "   ·473   11·30 "
     1969 .   .   ·472   11·57 "
     1969 .   "   ·472   11·57 .
     1944 "   11·46 "
M.V. = 1974 f.s.

   In round figures the Ballistics might
be described as 2000 Velocity at 12 tons,
pressure, certainly the best results given
in this barrel.
                        signed (F.W.J.)

Appendix V

References

Dedication *A History of Firearms*, by H. B. C. Pollard, London 1926.

Chapter 1

9 An account of the centenary dinner was given in *The Shooting Times* of the period.

9 Manton's life is described in a number of books, notably *The Mantons: Gunmakers*, by W. Keith Neil and D. H. L. Black, published by Herbert Jenkins 1967.

10 The lives of the early gunmakers is taken from G. T. Teasdale-Buckell's *Experts on Guns and Shooting*, London 1900.

10 The relative's letter is in possession of Mr Gavin Johnston. Other Holland letters quoted in this chapter are in the Holland archives.

17 The description of Henry Holland is taken from Teasdale-Buckell *op cit*.

22 The descriptions of the guns and those in Chapter 3 were initially written by Mr Carey Keates in 1976 and published by Holland & Holland, and in 1985 revised and updated by Mr Jeremy Clowes and Mr David Winks of Holland & Holland.

Chapter 2

31 The comprehensive book by de Witt Bailey and Douglas A. Nie can be complemented by accounts in the Teasdale-Buckell book above.

31 Sir Ralph's quotation is from the *Badminton* article quoted more fully in Chapter 8.

34 Col. Hawker's *Instructions to Young Sportsmen*, London 1814.

Chapter 3

38 *The Field* has kindly supplied photocopies of the reports of the trials in their issues of 1883.

39 Teasdale-Buckell *op cit*.

40 W. W. Greener whose *The Gun and its Development* was published London 1881.

Chapter 4

46 *Purdey's*, by The Hon. Richard Beaumont published by David & Charles 1984.

47 *The British Sniper 1915–83*, Ian Skennerton, published Arms and Armour Press 1984.

53 This information about the numbers of sniping guns was supplied by Mr. Laidler.

Chapter 5

55 *The Westley Richards Firm 1812–1913*, by Leslie B. Taylor, published by Shakespeare Head Press 1913.

56 The extensive quotations from Mr Malcolm Lyell are taken from a fuller manuscript of his in the Holland & Holland archives.

Chapter 6

71 Mr Geoffrey Brooks and Mr Russell Wilkin of Holland & Holland provided material for this section, as did Mr David Winks.

85 Since this chapter went to press a letter was received from Mr John Ross who joined Holland & Holland as an apprentice in July 1914 and whose grandfather 'old John Ross' was foreman of the action filing shop in the early days. Mr Ross's father and his brother George were also with the firm, the father retiring at 68 years old after 45 years of service. Thus, the Ross's accumulated memories probably go back to the 1860s and Mr Ross has confirmed several incidents mentioned in the book.

Chapter 7

86 Mr Alfred Bedford supplied the information on the London Proof House and quotations are taken from the *History of the Gunmaker's Association* and their *Notes on the Rules of Proof*. Further information on the Birmingham Proof House can be found in *The History of the Birmingham Gun-Barrel Proof House*, edited by Clive Harris, published by the Guardians of the Birmingham Proof House, 1946.

Chapter 8

92 *Shooting, Field and Covert*, Longman, Green & Co 1889.

92 Payne-Gallwey's article was printed in Vol. III of *The Badminton Magazine of Sports and Pastimes July to Dec 1896*, London 1896.

103 *Letters to Young Shooters*, London 1890 (First Series) 1894 (Second Series) 1896 (Third Series).

Chapter 9

105 This quotation from the *Evening Standard* undated, is in the Holland archives.

106 Lady Diana Cooper *The Rainbow Comes and Goes*, London 1958.

110 Col. Hawker's *Instructions to Young sportsmen*, Macdonald Hastings *The Shotgun*, David & Charles 1981. *op cit*.

110 The copy in the Holland & Holland archives has on the spine the title *Hawker on Shooting*.

Chapter 10

114 Lady Diana Cooper *The Rainbow Comes and Goes, op cit.*

114 The popular book *The Big Shots*, by John Garnier Ruffer, Debrett's 1977 mistakenly refers to the Duke of Portland as the 5th Duke whereas this was the eccentric father of the 'great shot' who was the 6th Duke. His book, *Men, Women & Things*, London 1939, is quoted extensively in the *Shooting and Deerstalking* volume of the series *British Sports & Sportsmen* series. The background to *The Big Shots* forms part of the film of Isabel Colegate's *The Shooting Party*, Hamish Hamilton 1980, which mentions Mr Holland's guns favourably.

116 The story about Willoughby is related in *The Big Shots*, p.47.

Chapter 11

125 De Witt Bailey and Douglas A. Nie, *op cit.*

126 Lady Jenkins *Sport and Travel in Both Tibets*, published London 1909.

128 William Howard Russell's book *With the Prince in India*, London 1877.

128 A. E. T. Watson *King Edward VII as a Sportsman*, London 1911 contains a chapter on the Prince of Wales's Indian Tour.

130–1 This account of cartridges in use was first published by Holland & Holland in 1976.

131 *Plain Tales from the Raj*, reprinted Century, 1985.

133 The picture of the Royal visit was provided by Photo Source.

134–6 Malcolm Lyell wrote an article in *The Times* on June 12th 1971 from which extracts are taken.

Chapter 12

137 Malcolm Lyell wrote this material which is supplemented by information published by Holland & Holland in 1976.

137 Lord Wolverton *Five Month's Sports in Somaliland*, London 1894.

139 Theodore Roosevelt *African Game Trails*, published by John Murray, London 1910.

139 F. C. Selous *Sport and Travel, East and West*, London & New York 1900 provides useful background.

140 L. H. Wilson *Theodore Roosevelt*, New York 1971.

140 The quotation from the bottom of the page is from W. W. Greener *op cit.*

141 Sir Samuel Baker: *The Rifle and the Hound in Ceylon*, London 1854 *Albert N'Yanza*, London 1866 *The Nile Tributaries of Abyssinia*, London 1870 *Ismailia*, London 1874.

143 Col. R. Meinertzhagen's book *Kenya Diary* has been republished by Eland 1985.

143 P. H. G. Powell-Cotton *Unknown Africa*, London 1904, and *A Sporting Trip through Abyssinia*, London 1902.

143 John Taylor *African Rifles and Cartridges*, Georgetown SC, 1948. He also wrote *Big Game and Big Game Rifles*, Herbert Jenkins 1948.

Chapter 13

147 Brian Jackman's account was published in *The Sunday Times*, in 1978.

149 These details of punt guns were published by Holland & Holland in 1976 in their notes on the Collections.

155 Sir Ralph Payne-Gallwey, Bart *The Fowler in Ireland*, London 1882.

Chapter 14

158 Malcolm Lyell's manuscript in the Holland archives.

160 These details of the commemorative guns were published by Holland & Holland in booklets to record each set.

170 A. I. Shand *The Gun Room*, London 1905.

Illustration Acknowledgements

Parker Gallery : 32 , 37 , 109 (both), 112–3, 154 .

Illustrated London News: 102, 110 (top), 117 (left), 118 (top), 119 (top), 122 (left), 123 , 130 , 132–3.

Mary Evans Picture Library: 40 , 96 , 108 , 110 (left and bottom right), 139 , 150 , 152 .

Imperial War Museum: 46 , 47 , 48 .

The Field: 38 .

Frost and Reed: front cover illustration (especial thanks for obtaining transparency from USA).

Simon Portal: 131

Commander John Anderton OBE, VRD: 114 .

Rodney Exton: 115 .

India Office, Curzon Collection: 131 (bottom), 134 .

Royal Geographical Society: 142

Malcolm Lyell: 33 , 100